EXAMINATION SERIES

This is your PASSBOOK® for...

Stock Clerk

Test Preparation Study Guide

Questions & Answers

Copyright © 2018 by

National Learning Corporation

212 Michael Drive, Syosset, New York 11791

All rights reserved, including the right of reproduction in whole or in part, in any form or by any means, electronic or mechanical, including photocopying, recording, or by any information storage and retrieval system, without permission in writing from the Publisher.

(516) 921-8888
(800) 632-8888
(800) 645-6337
FAX: (516) 921-8743
www.passbooks.com
info @ passbooks.com

PRINTED IN THE UNITED STATES OF AMERICA

PASSBOOK®
NOTICE

This book is SOLELY intended for, is sold ONLY to, and its use is RESTRICTED to *individual*, bona fide applicants or candidates who qualify by virtue of having seriously filed applications for appropriate license, certificate, professional and/or promotional advancement, higher school matriculation, scholarship, or other legitimate requirements of educational and/or governmental authorities.

This book is NOT intended for use, class instruction, tutoring, training, duplication, copying, reprinting, excerption, or adaptation, etc., by:

(1) Other publishers

(2) Proprietors and/or Instructors of "Coaching" and/or Preparatory Courses

(3) Personnel and/or Training Divisions of commercial, industrial, and governmental organizations

(4) Schools, colleges, or universities and/or their departments and staffs, including teachers and other personnel

(5) Testing Agencies or Bureaus

(6) Study groups which seek by the purchase of a single volume to copy and/or duplicate and/or adapt this material for use by the group as a whole without having purchased individual volumes for each of the members of the group

(7) Et al.

Such persons would be in violation of appropriate Federal and State statutes.

PROVISION OF LICENSING AGREEMENTS. — Recognized educational commercial, industrial, and governmental institutions and organizations, and others legitimately engaged in educational pursuits, including training, testing, and measurement activities, may address a request for a licensing agreement to the copyright owners, who will determine whether, and under what conditions, including fees and charges, the materials in this book may be used by them. In other words, a licensing facility exists for the legitimate use of the material in this book on other than an individual basis. However, it is asseverated and affirmed here that the material in this book *CANNOT* be used without the receipt of the express permission of such a licensing agreement from the Publishers.

NATIONAL LEARNING CORPORATION
212 Michael Drive
Syosset, New York 11791

Inquiries re licensing agreements should be addressed to:
The President
National Learning Corporation
212 Michael Drive
Syosset, New York 11791

PASSBOOK® SERIES

THE *PASSBOOK® SERIES* has been created to prepare applicants and candidates for the ultimate academic battlefield – the examination room.

At some time in our lives, each and every one of us may be required to take an examination – for validation, matriculation, admission, qualification, registration, certification, or licensure.

Based on the assumption that every applicant or candidate has met the basic formal educational standards, has taken the required number of courses, and read the necessary texts, the *PASSBOOK® SERIES* furnishes the one special preparation which may assure passing with confidence, instead of failing with insecurity. Examination questions – together with answers – are furnished as the basic vehicle for study so that the mysteries of the examination and its compounding difficulties may be eliminated or diminished by a sure method.

This book is meant to help you pass your examination provided that you qualify and are serious in your objective.

The entire field is reviewed through the huge store of content information which is succinctly presented through a provocative and challenging approach – the question-and-answer method.

A climate of success is established by furnishing the correct answers at the end of each test.

You soon learn to recognize types of questions, forms of questions, and patterns of questioning. You may even begin to anticipate expected outcomes.

You perceive that many questions are repeated or adapted so that you can gain acute insights, which may enable you to score many sure points.

You learn how to confront new questions, or types of questions, and to attack them confidently and work out the correct answers.

You note objectives and emphases, and recognize pitfalls and dangers, so that you may make positive educational adjustments.

Moreover, you are kept fully informed in relation to new concepts, methods, practices, and directions in the field.

You discover that you are actually taking the examination all the time: you are preparing for the examination by "taking" an examination, not by reading extraneous and/or supererogatory textbooks.

In short, this PASSBOOK®, used directedly, should be an important factor in helping you to pass your test.

STOCK CLERK

DUTIES
Performs routine manual and minor clerical work in receiving, storing, and dispensing supplies in a storeroom of a department or jurisdiction. Receives, unpacks, and stores goods and supplies in proper areas; assists in checking incoming materials against invoices or purchase orders or in filling requisitions. Maintains varied stock records such as bin and perpetual inventory cards. Assembles, packs, and transports, or arranges for transporting, stored goods or materials. Performs related work as required.

SCOPE OF THE EXAMINATION
The written test will cover knowledge, skills, and/or abilities in such areas as:
1. Storekeeping and inventory control;
2. Keeping simple inventory records;
3. Understanding and intepreting written material;
4. Name and number checking;
5. Coding; and
6. Arithmetic computation.

HOW TO PREPARE GUIDE FOR STOCK CLERK WRITTEN EXAMINATION

I. THE JOB

This is routine manual and clerical work in the operation of a small departmental supply unit. Employees in this class perform manual and clerical tasks in the receiving, stocking, and shipping of office, laboratory, hospital, and automotive supplies. An administrative supervisor assigns and reviews work on completion.

Work involves checking and recording receipt of supplies; stocking supplies in proper storage area; pulling supplies to fill orders, checking for required commodity, size, and amount; signing delivery tickets; packing supplies for shipment; storing and maintaining supplies; maintaining records; filling out requisitions for replenishing stock; and taking inventory of stock as required.

II. THE EXAMINATION

The examination for this classification is a multiple-choice exam. This multiple-choice exam is designed to measure specific knowledges and abilities. The test is divided into ten sections with each section measuring a different knowledge or ability. Applicants are presented with a test question and four possible responses to that question. Applicants then select the BEST possible response to the question.

During the exam, you will be required to respond to approximately 100 questions regarding ten topics. You will have three (3) hours to respond to the items.

III. HOW THE WRITTEN EXAMINATION WAS DEVELOPED

A study of the Stock Clerk classification was conducted before developing the examination. Employees who work in this position and their supervisors participated in this study to determine what job duties are performed by Stock Clerks and what knowledges and abilities a Stock Clerk must possess in order to perform these job duties.

When the study was completed, the results showed that a new employee in the position of Stock Clerk must be able to perform the activities listed below.

- Performs record keeping/reporting duties using personal computer, fax machine, card system, forms, logs and files following departmental guidelines and procedures and own initiative in order to maintain documentation of transactions, determine if balances on hand are up-to-date, and use as reference in determining estimates for future purchases.

The study also showed that the following knowledges and abilities are associated with the above activity. A Stock Clerk must possess the knowledges and abilities listed below their first day of work before training:

- **Ability to write correspondence such as letters, memos, reports, and summaries as needed to provide and document information.**

- **Ability to conduct inventories to include locating supplies and equipment, counting items, performing adjustments, and calculating quantities as needed to account for the inventory on records and obtain current balance.**

- Ability to write/print legibly as needed to record records, and document items issued from storeroom or warehouse on approved requisitions.

- Ability to establish minimum and maximum stock levels as needed to determine reorder points and add/delete items from stock.

- **Ability to file/retrieve documents using formats such as alphabetical, numerical, or alpha-numeric in order to store and retrieve the hard copy of documents.**

- Ability to operate a personal computer to include capabilities and software applications as needed to document and access information, transmit information, store and analyze information, and process reports.

- **Ability to read and comprehend narrative information such as catalogs, letters, checklists, memorandums, summaries, reports, contracts, and bid specifications as needed to make revisions, gain knowledge and understanding, ensure compliance with rules and regulations, and plan for future requirements and needs.**

- Ability to operate standard office equipment such as copier, shredder, telephone, fax machine, and typewriter to include purpose, capabilities, mechanics (preventive maintenance), and limitations as needed to maximize work time, receive and transmit information, and store and analyze information.

- Ability to communicate orally in one-on-one situations with departmental personnel and vendors as needed to ascertain the description of item needed, when equipment or supplies will be needed or delivered, vendor quotes, and equipment/supply availability and exchange information.

- Ability to count visually items on hand as needed to verify number of items received, pack requested items, and conduct physical inventory of items in stock.

- **Ability to plan/organize to include time management as needed to meet deadlines, allocate resources, and achieve objectives.**

- **Ability to prioritize tasks as needed to meet deadlines, allocate resources, and achieve objectives.**

- Ability to locate supplies within the stockroom or warehouse using commodity number, part number, or item description as needed to retrieve needed items and to search for lost or misplaced items.

- Ability to establish and maintain effective working relationships with individuals and groups such as co-workers, superiors, vendors, public officials, outside agencies, and the general public as needed to promote teamwork, enhance morale, improve performance, and communicate and achieve departmental goals.

- **Ability to follow written instructions as needed to accomplish assigned tasks and responsibilities.**

- **Ability to compare actual items and counts of items received with item description and counts printed on invoice or contract as needed to ensure order is correct.**

- **Ability to review printouts or computer screens in order to compare current inventory levels with reorder points as needed to determine which supplies should be reordered.**

- Ability to bend or stoop as needed to conduct inventories and move or carry shipments from shipping-and-receiving platform to storage or work area.

- **Ability to maintain records, either manually or electronically, of all property issued as needed to document to whom the property is issued.**

- Ability to manage multiple work orders simultaneously as needed to issue supplies and/or equipment in a timely manner and ensure supplies and equipment are charged to correct work order/account.

- Ability to follow oral instructions as needed to accomplish assigned tasks and responsibilities.

- Ability to apply rules, regulations, policies, and procedures to work performed as needed to organize work and make appropriate decisions concerning warehouse operations.

- Ability to give oral instructions as needed to accomplish assigned tasks and responsibilities.

- **Ability to compare part numbers consisting of numbers and/or number letter combinations as needed to determine if the numbers being compared are the same.**

- **Knowledge of basic math to include addition, subtraction, multiplication, and division as needed to order supplies, conduct inventories, calculate costs, and compose reports.**

- Knowledge of office supplies such as paper, writing instruments, correction fluids, etc. to include types, purpose, availability of state contracts, and quantity and sizes available as needed to issue and order supplies.

- **Knowledge of shipping/receiving procedures as needed to reconcile purchase orders to packing slip, inspect for damage, determine cost effective shipping method, and enter quantities into stock.**

IV. HOW TO PREPARE USING THIS GUIDE

This Pretest Booklet can be used as a practice guide. The questions contained in the booklet are a representation of some questions that will be on the actual examination. Familiarize yourself with the sample questions that follow. You would be well-advised to read the instructions and answer each question carefully. Like the examination questions (all of which are multiple choice), the sample items are presented in the following categories:

Section I:	Ability to Write Correspondence
Section II:	Ability to Conduct Inventories
Section III:	Ability to File/Retrieve Documents Ability to Maintain Records, Either Manually or Electronically, of all Property Issued
Section IV:	Ability to Read and Comprehend Narrative Information
Section V:	Ability to Plan/Organize Ability to Prioritize Tasks
Section VI:	Ability to Follow Written Instructions
Section VII:	Ability to Compare Part Numbers Consisting of Numbers and/or Number Letter Combinations
Section VIII:	Knowledge of Basic Math
Section IX:	Ability to Compare Actual Items and Counts of Items Received with Item Description and Counts Printed on Invoice or Contract Ability to Review Printouts or Computer Screens
Section X:	Knowledge of Shipping/Receiving Procedures

The sample items which follow are representative of the type of items that will appear on the exam. They are not necessarily based on the same information, diagrams, etc. as the actual exam. All questions will be multiple choice.

In addition, please review the General Instructions to Candidates Taking Written Examinations provided at the exam site on the day of the test.

V. SAMPLE TEST QUESTIONS

Section I: Ability to Write

Questions 1-5.

DIRECTIONS: In answering Questions 1 through 5, choose the correct answer.

1.
   A. You were setting there when I lay the two-way radio down.
   B. You were setting there when I laid the two-way radio down.
   C. You were sitting there when I lay the two-way radio down.
   D. You were sitting there when I laid the two-way radio down.

   1.____

2.
   A. It is imperative that the owner effect the changes now.
   B. It is imperative that the owner affect the changes now.
   C. It is imperative that the owner effects the changes now.
   D. It is imperative that the owner affects the changes now.

   2.____

3.
   A. It is the director's orders that he reports each violation of this rule immediately.
   B. It is orders of the director that he report all violations immediately of this rule.
   C. It is the director's order that he report immediately each violation of this rule.
   D. It is the director's order that he immediately reports every violation to this rule.

   3.____

4.
   A. John is better in arithmetic than I.
   B. John is better in arithmetic than me.
   C. John is more better in arithmetic than I.
   D. John is more better in arithmetic than me.

   4.____

5.
   A. The supervisor and the aide, together with the rest of the office force, has unanimously agreed to send a representative.
   B. The supervisor, together with the aide and the rest of the office force, have unanimously agreed to send a representative.
   C. The entire office force, including the supervisor and the aide, have unanimously agreed to send a representative.
   D. The entire office force, including the supervisor and the aide, has unanimously agreed to send a representative.

   5.____

Section II: Ability to Conduct Inventories

6. The beginning monthly inventory of hanging file folders is 657 boxes. You receive an order for 320 boxes of hanging file folders during the month. During the month, you ship 54 boxes of hanging file folders to field offices. What is the ending monthly balance of hanging file folders in inventory?
   A. 337
   B. 923
   C. 977
   D. None of the above

   6.____

7. A case contains six 5" x 8" legal pads. Your beginning balance was 17 cases of 5" x 8" legal pads. However, you distribute 86 pads to the Legal Division. How many pads do you have left?
   A. 0
   B. 10
   C. 11
   D. None of the above

   7._____

8. The beginning monthly inventory of dot matrix printers was 12. You shipped some of the dot matrix printers to surplus during the month. You received 12 dot matrix printers from the satellite offices. The ending monthly inventory is 12. How many dot matrix printers did you ship to surplus?
   A. 0
   B. 12
   C. 24
   D. None of the above

   8._____

Section III: Ability to File/Retrieve Documents/Maintain Records

Questions 9-11.

DIRECTIONS: The drawers of a four-drawing filing cabinet are designated 1, 2, 3, and 4, with the top drawer being 1 and the bottom 4. Folders are filed in these drawers in accordance with the following alphabetical index:

   Drawer 1:   By last name in files labeled A through G
   Drawer 2:   By last name in files labeled H through N
   Drawer 3:   By last name in files labeled O through T
   Drawer 4:   By last name in files labeled U through Z

9. Aaron J. Smith's folder should be filed in Drawer
   A. 1   B. 2   C. 3   D. 4

   9._____

10. Ricky R. Williams' folder should be filed in Drawer
    A. 1   B. 2   C. 3   D. 4

    10._____

11. Diana Thomas' folder should be filed in Drawer
    A. 1   B. 2   C. 3   D. 4

    11._____

Section IV: Ability to Read and Comprehend Narrative Information

Questions 12-13.

DIRECTIONS: Questions 12 and 13 are based on the following reading passage.

Laboratory Stockroom Safety

One of the basic pre-requisites to working safely in the lab stockroom is to know as much as possible about the substances, processes, and equipment being used. In fact, you have a right to know, under the Laboratory Safety Standard about the hazardous substances you handle. There are varieties of resources available to you for lab safety information, including:

Section Supervisor: Should inform you about the Chemical Hygiene Plan, and the hazards/safety precautions for all activities you will be conducting or supervising.

Chemical Hygiene Plan: Each lab supervisor (Chemical Hygiene Officer) must have and share with their employees their lab-specific Chemical Hygiene Plan. It should provide the basic procedures and resources necessary for effective chemical safety information and training.

Hazard Communication Coordinator (HCC): Each department has an HCC to assist you in answering general safety questions about your department, obtaining MSDS and acting as contact to EH&S.

Material Safety Data Sheets (MSDS): Are chemical information forms which manufacturers of hazardous substances must make available to those who purchase their products.

Reference Books/Videos: A list of recommended safety references and videos are available from your supervisor. The reference books may be available in your department or the library, or they can be used by employees for research at the EH&S office. The videos listed are available on a free five-day rental basis from EH&S (534-3766).

EH&S Staff: Environmental Health & Safety can provide information or help answer questions about many safety-related issues. Call 534-7534 for further information.

The Occupational Safety and Training Division: Can provide educational materials and other training aids/courses. A summary of the regular training programs provided by EH&S is available upon request. Some courses/materials are already prepared or on hand and can be obtained by calling EH&S. Other needs may not be available through EH&S, but can typically be arranged through this office. Special rates may also be available through EH&S. Call 534-3766 for additional information.

12. According to the above passage, the Hazard Communication Coordinator is responsible for   12._____
    A. responding to safety questions, obtaining Material Safety Data Sheets, and acting as liaison to EH&S
    B. communicating procedures and sharing resources on chemical protection information and training
    C. providing laboratory safety educational materials and other training aids/courses
    D. coordinating the activities of the Occupational Safety and Training Division

13. Safety videos are available from the   13._____
    A. Environmental Health & Safety Staff
    B. section supervisor
    C. Occupational Safety and Training Division
    D. Hazard Communication Coordinator

Section V: Ability to Plan/Organize/Prioritize Tasks

Questions 14-16.

DIRECTIONS: Read the passage and then answer Questions 14 through 16. You may refer to the passage when answering the questions.

As a Stock Clerk, you spend exactly two (2) hours each day filing. There are three types of documents that you file, and each has its own priority. Review the following information about the filing work, and then respond to Questions 14 through 16.

Supply Requisition Form is of top priority. Filing of these documents must occur daily. They are filed in Room 235.

ESP-100 Form is of medium priority. Filing of these documents must occur within three days. These documents are filed in Room 400-A. It takes half the time to file a single ESP-100 as it takes to file a single Supply Requisition Form.

TP-007 is of low priority. Filing of these documents must occur within one work week. They are filed in Room 430-B. It takes four times as long to file a single TP-007 as it takes to file a Supply Requisition Form.

14. Today is Monday. You have 100 Supply Requisition Forms to file, 200 ESP-100 forms, and 400 TP-007 forms. If you can file 100 Supply Requisition Forms in one hour, which of the following is the MOST efficient use of your time for the day?
    A. File all Supply Requisition Forms and all ESP-100 forms
    B. File all Supply Requisition Forms
    C. File all ESP-100 forms and all TP-007 forms
    D. File all TP-007 forms

    14.____

15. Assume that it takes one hour to file 100 Supply Requisition Forms. If you have 150 Supply Requisition Forms to file, which of the following could be completed the same day?
    A. 100 ESP-100 forms   B. 50 ESP-100 forms
    C. 25 TP-007 forms   D. 50 TP-007 forms

    15.____

16. You have 50 TP-007 forms to file. If this takes you one hour, how many Supply Requisition Forms could you file that same day?
    A. 50   B. 100   C. 200   D. 250

    16.____

Section VI: Ability to Follow Written Instructions

Questions 17-19.

DIRECTIONS: Questions 17 through 19 are based on the following reading passage.

Travel Accounts/Definitions – Employee Travel

Travel accounts are defined based on destination:

In-state: The destination of the trip must be located within the boundaries of the State.

Out-of-State: The destination of the trip must be located outside the boundaries of the State. Travel to Canada, Alaska, Hawaii, or to the U.S. territories and possessions is considered out-of-state travel.

Out-of-Country: The destination of the trip must be located outside the boundaries of Canada and the United States and its territories and possessions.

Transportation Accounts

These subsidiary accounts include the cost of proceeding from one place to another while in travel status. Transportation expenses include automobile allowances, airplane, train, bus, taxicab, limousine, subway, streetcar fares, rental car and motor pool charges and parking and toll fees. Taxicab gratuities are also included.

	In-State	Out-of-State	Out-of-Country
Air	53111	53121	53131
Ground	53112	53122	53132

Subsistence Accounts

These subsidiary accounts include the cost of obtaining basic provisions in the form of food and shelter while in travel status. Subsistence expenses include the cost of breakfast, lunch, dinner and lodging and the per diem allowances. Food cost is inclusive of gratuities and taxes.

	In-State	Out-of-State	Out-of-Country
Lodging	53114	53124	53134
Meals	53115	53125	53135

Other Travel Expenses

These subsidiary accounts include the cost incurred while in travel status for services and/or goods other than for transportation, registration, and subsistence. Other travel expenses include the cost of miscellaneous telephone charges and supplies, baggage handling gratuities, and other appropriate items.

	In-State	Out-of-State	Out-of-Country
Telephone/Misc.	53116	53126	53136

Registration Accounts

These subsidiary accounts include the fees for registration for a conference, convention, meeting, seminar, workshop, and training. All fees should be paid directly to the organization/vendor using the Small Purchase Process.

	In-State	Out-of-State	Out-of-Country
Conference	53119	53129	53139
Workshop/Trng.	53951	53951	53951

17. What would be the Transportation Account code number for an employee traveling from Huntsville, Alabama to Mobile, Alabama using an automobile?   17.____
    A. 53112   B. 53121   C. 53111   D. 53122

18. What would be the Registration Account code number for an employee traveling from Monroeville, Alabama to Atlanta, Georgia to attend a workshop?   18.____
    A. 53112   B. 53121   C. 53111   D. 53951

19. What would be the Transportation Account code number for an employee traveling from Huntsville, Alabama to Chattanooga, Tennessee using an automobile?   19.____
    A. 53112   B. 53121   C. 53111   D. 53122

Section VII: Ability to Compare Part Numbers Consisting of Numbers and/or Number Letter Combinations

Questions 20-21.

DIRECTIONS: In this section, there are questions that involve data comparison. Your task is to determine the number of identical pairs of names and numbers in each list. Then select the correct answer using the KEY below.

KEY

A = There is only one (1) set of identical pairs.
B = There are two (2) sets of identical pairs.
C = There are three (3) sets of identical pairs.
D = There are four (4) sets of identical pairs.

20. Original
    34567839030
    Isabella Office
    The Robin's Suite
    St. Eleanora's Office
    James A. Moore Office

    Copy
    Pelam Office
    Isabela Office
    The Roben's Suite
    St. Eleanora's Office
    James A. More Office

    20.____

21. Original
    33423
    7362AZ
    7362536478ZHBC
    7362819273HDBC
    27364829304812

    Copy
    33423
    7363AZ
    7362536478ZHBC
    7362819273HDBC
    27364829304812

    21.____

Section VIII: Knowledge of Basic Math

DIRECTIONS: Calculate the following.

22. 90% of 82 is what number?
    A. 80.7   B. 73.8   C. 75.4   D. 88.3

    22.____

23. Thirty-seven percent of 82,600 is equal to
    A. 27,560   B. 28,075   C. 29,550   D. 30,562

    23.____

24. Fees collected for annual permits increased from $22,464.00 to $24,710.40 last year. If it is increased by the same percent this year, what will be the amount of fees collected?
    A. $26,782.64   B. $27,181.44   C. $27,438.52   D. $27,982.64

    24.____

Section IX: Ability to Compare Actual Items and Counts of Items/Review Printouts or Computer Screens

Questions 25-26.

DIRECTIONS: Use the invoice below to respond to Questions 25 and 26.

INVOICE

Stock #	Description	Unit	Price/Unit	No. of Units	Total
WER-9418833	Electric Stapler	each	$44.25	8	$354.00
RED-7408682	Adjustable 3-Hole Punch	each	$9.90	16	$158.40
CEV-7265286	Heavy-Duty Binders	each	$7.15	24	$171.60
QSE-8505724	Small Colored Binder Clips	36/Pack	$4.59	32	$146.88
GEH-61399049	Rubber Bands	1 lb box	$5.69	48	$273.12

PACKING SLIP

Stock #	Item Description	# Shipped
RED-7408682	Adjustable 5-Hole Punch	16

25. Based on the information provided on the packing slip above,
    A. There is a discrepancy between the number of items shipped and the number of items ordered.
    B. The description of item shipped does not match the description of the item ordered.
    C. The stock number does not match the stock number of the item ordered.
    D. The product was shipped as ordered.

    25.____

PACKING SLIP

Stock #	Item Description	# Shipped
QSE-8505724	Small Colored Binder Clips	36

26. Based on the information provided on the packing slip above, 26.____
    A. There is a discrepancy between the number of items shipped and the number of items ordered.
    B. The description of item shipped does not match the description of the item ordered.
    C. The stock number does not match the stock number of the item ordered.
    D. The product was shipped as ordered.

Section X: Knowledge of Shipping/Receiving Procedures

27. The amount for which a package is protected against loss or damage 27.____
    is called
    A. insured value   B. net worth
    C. declared value   D. in transit bond

28. A container that contains multiple units of an item is called a 28.____
    A. gross   B. carton   C. case   D. bin

29. The process of removing materials from stock and transporting them 29.____
    to a customer or another facility is called
    A. transporting   B. shipping
    C. shrinkage   D. freight

KEY (CORRECT ANSWERS)

1.	D	11.	C	21.	D
2.	A	12.	A	22.	B
3.	C	13.	A	23.	D
4.	A	14.	A	24.	B
5.	D	15.	B	25.	B
6.	B	16.	C	26.	A
7.	D	17.	A	27.	A
8.	B	18.	D	28.	C
9.	C	19.	D	29.	B
10.	D	20.	A		

HOW TO TAKE A TEST

I. YOU MUST PASS AN EXAMINATION

A. *WHAT EVERY CANDIDATE SHOULD KNOW*

Examination applicants often ask us for help in preparing for the written test. What can I study in advance? What kinds of questions will be asked? How will the test be given? How will the papers be graded?

As an applicant for a civil service examination, you may be wondering about some of these things. Our purpose here is to suggest effective methods of advance study and to describe civil service examinations.

Your chances for success on this examination can be increased if you know how to prepare. Those "pre-examination jitters" can be reduced if you know what to expect. You can even experience an adventure in good citizenship if you know why civil service exams are given.

B. *WHY ARE CIVIL SERVICE EXAMINATIONS GIVEN?*

Civil service examinations are important to you in two ways. As a citizen, you want public jobs filled by employees who know how to do their work. As a job seeker, you want a fair chance to compete for that job on an equal footing with other candidates. The best-known means of accomplishing this two-fold goal is the competitive examination.

Exams are widely publicized throughout the nation. They may be administered for jobs in federal, state, city, municipal, town or village governments or agencies.

Any citizen may apply, with some limitations, such as the age or residence of applicants. Your experience and education may be reviewed to see whether you meet the requirements for the particular examination. When these requirements exist, they are reasonable and applied consistently to all applicants. Thus, a competitive examination may cause you some uneasiness now, but it is your privilege and safeguard.

C. *HOW ARE CIVIL SERVICE EXAMS DEVELOPED?*

Examinations are carefully written by trained technicians who are specialists in the field known as "psychological measurement," in consultation with recognized authorities in the field of work that the test will cover. These experts recommend the subject matter areas or skills to be tested; only those knowledges or skills important to your success on the job are included. The most reliable books and source materials available are used as references. Together, the experts and technicians judge the difficulty level of the questions.

Test technicians know how to phrase questions so that the problem is clearly stated. Their ethics do not permit "trick" or "catch" questions. Questions may have been tried out on sample groups, or subjected to statistical analysis, to determine their usefulness.

Written tests are often used in combination with performance tests, ratings of training and experience, and oral interviews. All of these measures combine to form the best-known means of finding the right person for the right job.

II. HOW TO PASS THE WRITTEN TEST

A. NATURE OF THE EXAMINATION

To prepare intelligently for civil service examinations, you should know how they differ from school examinations you have taken. In school you were assigned certain definite pages to read or subjects to cover. The examination questions were quite detailed and usually emphasized memory. Civil service exams, on the other hand, try to discover your present ability to perform the duties of a position, plus your potentiality to learn these duties. In other words, a civil service exam attempts to predict how successful you will be. Questions cover such a broad area that they cannot be as minute and detailed as school exam questions.

In the public service similar kinds of work, or positions, are grouped together in one "class." This process is known as *position-classification*. All the positions in a class are paid according to the salary range for that class. One class title covers all of these positions, and they are all tested by the same examination.

B. FOUR BASIC STEPS

1) Study the announcement

How, then, can you know what subjects to study? Our best answer is: "Learn as much as possible about the class of positions for which you've applied." The exam will test the knowledge, skills and abilities needed to do the work.

Your most valuable source of information about the position you want is the official exam announcement. This announcement lists the training and experience qualifications. Check these standards and apply only if you come reasonably close to meeting them.

The brief description of the position in the examination announcement offers some clues to the subjects which will be tested. Think about the job itself. Review the duties in your mind. Can you perform them, or are there some in which you are rusty? Fill in the blank spots in your preparation.

Many jurisdictions preview the written test in the exam announcement by including a section called "Knowledge and Abilities Required," "Scope of the Examination," or some similar heading. Here you will find out specifically what fields will be tested.

2) Review your own background

Once you learn in general what the position is all about, and what you need to know to do the work, ask yourself which subjects you already know fairly well and which need improvement. You may wonder whether to concentrate on improving your strong areas or on building some background in your fields of weakness. When the announcement has specified "some knowledge" or "considerable knowledge," or has used adjectives like "beginning principles of…" or "advanced … methods," you can get a clue as to the number and difficulty of questions to be asked in any given field. More questions, and hence broader coverage, would be included for those subjects which are more important in the work. Now weigh your strengths and weaknesses against the job requirements and prepare accordingly.

3) Determine the level of the position

Another way to tell how intensively you should prepare is to understand the level of the job for which you are applying. Is it the entering level? In other words, is this the position in which beginners in a field of work are hired? Or is it an intermediate or advanced level? Sometimes this is indicated by such words as "Junior" or "Senior" in the class title. Other jurisdictions use Roman numerals to designate the level – Clerk I, Clerk II, for example. The word "Supervisor" sometimes appears in the title. If the level is not indicated by the title, check the description of duties. Will you be working under very close supervision, or will you have responsibility for independent decisions in this work?

4) Choose appropriate study materials

Now that you know the subjects to be examined and the relative amount of each subject to be covered, you can choose suitable study materials. For beginning level jobs, or even advanced ones, if you have a pronounced weakness in some aspect of your training, read a modern, standard textbook in that field. Be sure it is up to date and has general coverage. Such books are normally available at your library, and the librarian will be glad to help you locate one. For entry-level positions, questions of appropriate difficulty are chosen – neither highly advanced questions, nor those too simple. Such questions require careful thought but not advanced training.

If the position for which you are applying is technical or advanced, you will read more advanced, specialized material. If you are already familiar with the basic principles of your field, elementary textbooks would waste your time. Concentrate on advanced textbooks and technical periodicals. Think through the concepts and review difficult problems in your field.

These are all general sources. You can get more ideas on your own initiative, following these leads. For example, training manuals and publications of the government agency which employs workers in your field can be useful, particularly for technical and professional positions. A letter or visit to the government department involved may result in more specific study suggestions, and certainly will provide you with a more definite idea of the exact nature of the position you are seeking.

III. KINDS OF TESTS

Tests are used for purposes other than measuring knowledge and ability to perform specified duties. For some positions, it is equally important to test ability to make adjustments to new situations or to profit from training. In others, basic mental abilities not dependent on information are essential. Questions which test these things may not appear as pertinent to the duties of the position as those which test for knowledge and information. Yet they are often highly important parts of a fair examination. For very general questions, it is almost impossible to help you direct your study efforts. What we can do is to point out some of the more common of these general abilities needed in public service positions and describe some typical questions.

1) General information

Broad, general information has been found useful for predicting job success in some kinds of work. This is tested in a variety of ways, from vocabulary lists to questions about current events. Basic background in some field of work, such as sociology or economics, may be sampled in a group of questions. Often these are principles which have become familiar to most persons through exposure rather than through formal training. It is difficult to advise you how to study for these questions; being alert to the world around you is our best suggestion.

2) Verbal ability

An example of an ability needed in many positions is verbal or language ability. Verbal ability is, in brief, the ability to use and understand words. Vocabulary and grammar tests are typical measures of this ability. Reading comprehension or paragraph interpretation questions are common in many kinds of civil service tests. You are given a paragraph of written material and asked to find its central meaning.

3) Numerical ability

Number skills can be tested by the familiar arithmetic problem, by checking paired lists of numbers to see which are alike and which are different, or by interpreting charts and graphs. In the latter test, a graph may be printed in the test booklet which you are asked to use as the basis for answering questions.

4) Observation

A popular test for law-enforcement positions is the observation test. A picture is shown to you for several minutes, then taken away. Questions about the picture test your ability to observe both details and larger elements.

5) Following directions

In many positions in the public service, the employee must be able to carry out written instructions dependably and accurately. You may be given a chart with several columns, each column listing a variety of information. The questions require you to carry out directions involving the information given in the chart.

6) Skills and aptitudes

Performance tests effectively measure some manual skills and aptitudes. When the skill is one in which you are trained, such as typing or shorthand, you can practice. These tests are often very much like those given in business school or high school courses. For many of the other skills and aptitudes, however, no short-time preparation can be made. Skills and abilities natural to you or that you have developed throughout your lifetime are being tested.

Many of the general questions just described provide all the data needed to answer the questions and ask you to use your reasoning ability to find the answers. Your best preparation for these tests, as well as for tests of facts and ideas, is to be at your physical and mental best. You, no doubt, have your own methods of getting into an exam-taking mood and keeping "in shape." The next section lists some ideas on this subject.

IV. KINDS OF QUESTIONS

Only rarely is the "essay" question, which you answer in narrative form, used in civil service tests. Civil service tests are usually of the short-answer type. Full instructions for answering these questions will be given to you at the examination. But in case this is your first experience with short-answer questions and separate answer sheets, here is what you need to know:

1) Multiple-choice Questions

Most popular of the short-answer questions is the "multiple choice" or "best answer" question. It can be used, for example, to test for factual knowledge, ability to solve problems or judgment in meeting situations found at work.

A multiple-choice question is normally one of three types—
- It can begin with an incomplete statement followed by several possible endings. You are to find the one ending which *best* completes the statement, although some of the others may not be entirely wrong.
- It can also be a complete statement in the form of a question which is answered by choosing one of the statements listed.

- It can be in the form of a problem – again you select the best answer.

Here is an example of a multiple-choice question with a discussion which should give you some clues as to the method for choosing the right answer:

When an employee has a complaint about his assignment, the action which will *best* help him overcome his difficulty is to
   A. discuss his difficulty with his coworkers
   B. take the problem to the head of the organization
   C. take the problem to the person who gave him the assignment
   D. say nothing to anyone about his complaint

In answering this question, you should study each of the choices to find which is best. Consider choice "A" – Certainly an employee may discuss his complaint with fellow employees, but no change or improvement can result, and the complaint remains unresolved. Choice "B" is a poor choice since the head of the organization probably does not know what assignment you have been given, and taking your problem to him is known as "going over the head" of the supervisor. The supervisor, or person who made the assignment, is the person who can clarify it or correct any injustice. Choice "C" is, therefore, correct. To say nothing, as in choice "D," is unwise. Supervisors have and interest in knowing the problems employees are facing, and the employee is seeking a solution to his problem.

2) True/False Questions

The "true/false" or "right/wrong" form of question is sometimes used. Here a complete statement is given. Your job is to decide whether the statement is right or wrong.

SAMPLE: A roaming cell-phone call to a nearby city costs less than a non-roaming call to a distant city.

This statement is wrong, or false, since roaming calls are more expensive.
This is not a complete list of all possible question forms, although most of the others are variations of these common types. You will always get complete directions for answering questions. Be sure you understand *how* to mark your answers – ask questions until you do.

V. RECORDING YOUR ANSWERS

Computer terminals are used more and more today for many different kinds of exams.
For an examination with very few applicants, you may be told to record your answers in the test booklet itself. Separate answer sheets are much more common. If this separate answer sheet is to be scored by machine – and this is often the case – it is highly important that you mark your answers correctly in order to get credit.
An electronic scoring machine is often used in civil service offices because of the speed with which papers can be scored. Machine-scored answer sheets must be marked with a pencil, which will be given to you. This pencil has a high graphite content which responds to the electronic scoring machine. As a matter of fact, stray dots may register as answers, so do not let your pencil rest on the answer sheet while you are pondering the correct answer. Also, if your pencil lead breaks or is otherwise defective, ask for another.

Since the answer sheet will be dropped in a slot in the scoring machine, be careful not to bend the corners or get the paper crumpled.

The answer sheet normally has five vertical columns of numbers, with 30 numbers to a column. These numbers correspond to the question numbers in your test booklet. After each number, going across the page are four or five pairs of dotted lines. These short dotted lines have small letters or numbers above them. The first two pairs may also have a "T" or "F" above the letters. This indicates that the first two pairs only are to be used if the questions are of the true-false type. If the questions are multiple choice, disregard the "T" and "F" and pay attention only to the small letters or numbers.

Answer your questions in the manner of the sample that follows:

32. The largest city in the United States is
    A. Washington, D.C.
    B. New York City
    C. Chicago
    D. Detroit
    E. San Francisco

1) Choose the answer you think is best. (New York City is the largest, so "B" is correct.)
2) Find the row of dotted lines numbered the same as the question you are answering. (Find row number 32)
3) Find the pair of dotted lines corresponding to the answer. (Find the pair of lines under the mark "B.")
4) Make a solid black mark between the dotted lines.

VI. BEFORE THE TEST

Common sense will help you find procedures to follow to get ready for an examination. Too many of us, however, overlook these sensible measures. Indeed, nervousness and fatigue have been found to be the most serious reasons why applicants fail to do their best on civil service tests. Here is a list of reminders:

- Begin your preparation early – Don't wait until the last minute to go scurrying around for books and materials or to find out what the position is all about.
- Prepare continuously – An hour a night for a week is better than an all-night cram session. This has been definitely established. What is more, a night a week for a month will return better dividends than crowding your study into a shorter period of time.
- Locate the place of the exam – You have been sent a notice telling you when and where to report for the examination. If the location is in a different town or otherwise unfamiliar to you, it would be well to inquire the best route and learn something about the building.
- Relax the night before the test – Allow your mind to rest. Do not study at all that night. Plan some mild recreation or diversion; then go to bed early and get a good night's sleep.
- Get up early enough to make a leisurely trip to the place for the test – This way unforeseen events, traffic snarls, unfamiliar buildings, etc. will not upset you.
- Dress comfortably – A written test is not a fashion show. You will be known by number and not by name, so wear something comfortable.

- Leave excess paraphernalia at home – Shopping bags and odd bundles will get in your way. You need bring only the items mentioned in the official notice you received; usually everything you need is provided. Do not bring reference books to the exam. They will only confuse those last minutes and be taken away from you when in the test room.
- Arrive somewhat ahead of time – If because of transportation schedules you must get there very early, bring a newspaper or magazine to take your mind off yourself while waiting.
- Locate the examination room – When you have found the proper room, you will be directed to the seat or part of the room where you will sit. Sometimes you are given a sheet of instructions to read while you are waiting. Do not fill out any forms until you are told to do so; just read them and be prepared.
- Relax and prepare to listen to the instructions
- If you have any physical problem that may keep you from doing your best, be sure to tell the test administrator. If you are sick or in poor health, you really cannot do your best on the exam. You can come back and take the test some other time.

VII. AT THE TEST

The day of the test is here and you have the test booklet in your hand. The temptation to get going is very strong. Caution! There is more to success than knowing the right answers. You must know how to identify your papers and understand variations in the type of short-answer question used in this particular examination. Follow these suggestions for maximum results from your efforts:

1) Cooperate with the monitor

The test administrator has a duty to create a situation in which you can be as much at ease as possible. He will give instructions, tell you when to begin, check to see that you are marking your answer sheet correctly, and so on. He is not there to guard you, although he will see that your competitors do not take unfair advantage. He wants to help you do your best.

2) Listen to all instructions

Don't jump the gun! Wait until you understand all directions. In most civil service tests you get more time than you need to answer the questions. So don't be in a hurry. Read each word of instructions until you clearly understand the meaning. Study the examples, listen to all announcements and follow directions. Ask questions if you do not understand what to do.

3) Identify your papers

Civil service exams are usually identified by number only. You will be assigned a number; you must not put your name on your test papers. Be sure to copy your number correctly. Since more than one exam may be given, copy your exact examination title.

4) Plan your time

Unless you are told that a test is a "speed" or "rate of work" test, speed itself is usually not important. Time enough to answer all the questions will be provided, but this does not mean that you have all day. An overall time limit has been set. Divide the total time (in minutes) by the number of questions to determine the approximate time you have for each question.

5) Do not linger over difficult questions

If you come across a difficult question, mark it with a paper clip (useful to have along) and come back to it when you have been through the booklet. One caution if you do this – be sure to skip a number on your answer sheet as well. Check often to be sure that you have not lost your place and that you are marking in the row numbered the same as the question you are answering.

6) Read the questions

Be sure you know what the question asks! Many capable people are unsuccessful because they failed to *read* the questions correctly.

7) Answer all questions

Unless you have been instructed that a penalty will be deducted for incorrect answers, it is better to guess than to omit a question.

8) Speed tests

It is often better NOT to guess on speed tests. It has been found that on timed tests people are tempted to spend the last few seconds before time is called in marking answers at random – without even reading them – in the hope of picking up a few extra points. To discourage this practice, the instructions may warn you that your score will be "corrected" for guessing. That is, a penalty will be applied. The incorrect answers will be deducted from the correct ones, or some other penalty formula will be used.

9) Review your answers

If you finish before time is called, go back to the questions you guessed or omitted to give them further thought. Review other answers if you have time.

10) Return your test materials

If you are ready to leave before others have finished or time is called, take ALL your materials to the monitor and leave quietly. Never take any test material with you. The monitor can discover whose papers are not complete, and taking a test booklet may be grounds for disqualification.

VIII. EXAMINATION TECHNIQUES

1) Read the general instructions carefully. These are usually printed on the first page of the exam booklet. As a rule, these instructions refer to the timing of the examination; the fact that you should not start work until the signal and must stop work at a signal, etc. If there are any *special* instructions, such as a choice of questions to be answered, make sure that you note this instruction carefully.

2) When you are ready to start work on the examination, that is as soon as the signal has been given, read the instructions to each question booklet, underline any key words or phrases, such as *least, best, outline, describe* and the like. In this way you will tend to answer as requested rather than discover on reviewing your paper that you *listed without describing*, that you selected the *worst* choice rather than the *best* choice, etc.

3) If the examination is of the objective or multiple-choice type – that is, each question will also give a series of possible answers: A, B, C or D, and you are called upon to select the best answer and write the letter next to that answer on your answer paper – it is advisable to start answering each question in turn. There may be anywhere from 50 to 100 such questions in the three or four hours allotted and you can see how much time would be taken if you read through all the questions before beginning to answer any. Furthermore, if you come across a question or group of questions which you know would be difficult to answer, it would undoubtedly affect your handling of all the other questions.

4) If the examination is of the essay type and contains but a few questions, it is a moot point as to whether you should read all the questions before starting to answer any one. Of course, if you are given a choice – say five out of seven and the like – then it is essential to read all the questions so you can eliminate the two that are most difficult. If, however, you are asked to answer all the questions, there may be danger in trying to answer the easiest one first because you may find that you will spend too much time on it. The best technique is to answer the first question, then proceed to the second, etc.

5) Time your answers. Before the exam begins, write down the time it started, then add the time allowed for the examination and write down the time it must be completed, then divide the time available somewhat as follows:
   - If 3-1/2 hours are allowed, that would be 210 minutes. If you have 80 objective-type questions, that would be an average of 2-1/2 minutes per question. Allow yourself no more than 2 minutes per question, or a total of 160 minutes, which will permit about 50 minutes to review.
   - If for the time allotment of 210 minutes there are 7 essay questions to answer, that would average about 30 minutes a question. Give yourself only 25 minutes per question so that you have about 35 minutes to review.

6) The most important instruction is to *read each question* and make sure you know what is wanted. The second most important instruction is to *time yourself properly* so that you answer every question. The third most important instruction is to *answer every question*. Guess if you have to but include something for each question. Remember that you will receive no credit for a blank and will probably receive some credit if you write something in answer to an essay question. If you guess a letter – say "B" for a multiple-choice question – you may have guessed right. If you leave a blank as an answer to a multiple-choice question, the examiners may respect your feelings but it will not add a point to your score. Some exams may penalize you for wrong answers, so in such cases *only*, you may not want to guess unless you have some basis for your answer.

7) Suggestions
   a. Objective-type questions
      1. Examine the question booklet for proper sequence of pages and questions
      2. Read all instructions carefully
      3. Skip any question which seems too difficult; return to it after all other questions have been answered
      4. Apportion your time properly; do not spend too much time on any single question or group of questions

5. Note and underline key words – *all, most, fewest, least, best, worst, same, opposite,* etc.
6. Pay particular attention to negatives
7. Note unusual option, e.g., unduly long, short, complex, different or similar in content to the body of the question
8. Observe the use of "hedging" words – *probably, may, most likely,* etc.
9. Make sure that your answer is put next to the same number as the question
10. Do not second-guess unless you have good reason to believe the second answer is definitely more correct
11. Cross out original answer if you decide another answer is more accurate; do not erase until you are ready to hand your paper in
12. Answer all questions; guess unless instructed otherwise
13. Leave time for review

   b. Essay questions
   1. Read each question carefully
   2. Determine exactly what is wanted. Underline key words or phrases.
   3. Decide on outline or paragraph answer
   4. Include many different points and elements unless asked to develop any one or two points or elements
   5. Show impartiality by giving pros and cons unless directed to select one side only
   6. Make and write down any assumptions you find necessary to answer the questions
   7. Watch your English, grammar, punctuation and choice of words
   8. Time your answers; don't crowd material

8) Answering the essay question

Most essay questions can be answered by framing the specific response around several key words or ideas. Here are a few such key words or ideas:

M's: manpower, materials, methods, money, management
P's: purpose, program, policy, plan, procedure, practice, problems, pitfalls, personnel, public relations

   a. Six basic steps in handling problems:
   1. Preliminary plan and background development
   2. Collect information, data and facts
   3. Analyze and interpret information, data and facts
   4. Analyze and develop solutions as well as make recommendations
   5. Prepare report and sell recommendations
   6. Install recommendations and follow up effectiveness

   b. Pitfalls to avoid
   1. *Taking things for granted* – A statement of the situation does not necessarily imply that each of the elements is necessarily true; for example, a complaint may be invalid and biased so that all that can be taken for granted is that a complaint has been registered

2. *Considering only one side of a situation* – Wherever possible, indicate several alternatives and then point out the reasons you selected the best one
3. *Failing to indicate follow up* – Whenever your answer indicates action on your part, make certain that you will take proper follow-up action to see how successful your recommendations, procedures or actions turn out to be
4. *Taking too long in answering any single question* – Remember to time your answers properly

IX. AFTER THE TEST

Scoring procedures differ in detail among civil service jurisdictions although the general principles are the same. Whether the papers are hand-scored or graded by machine we have described, they are nearly always graded by number. That is, the person who marks the paper knows only the number – never the name – of the applicant. Not until all the papers have been graded will they be matched with names. If other tests, such as training and experience or oral interview ratings have been given, scores will be combined. Different parts of the examination usually have different weights. For example, the written test might count 60 percent of the final grade, and a rating of training and experience 40 percent. In many jurisdictions, veterans will have a certain number of points added to their grades.

After the final grade has been determined, the names are placed in grade order and an eligible list is established. There are various methods for resolving ties between those who get the same final grade – probably the most common is to place first the name of the person whose application was received first. Job offers are made from the eligible list in the order the names appear on it. You will be notified of your grade and your rank as soon as all these computations have been made. This will be done as rapidly as possible.

People who are found to meet the requirements in the announcement are called "eligibles." Their names are put on a list of eligible candidates. An eligible's chances of getting a job depend on how high he stands on this list and how fast agencies are filling jobs from the list.

When a job is to be filled from a list of eligibles, the agency asks for the names of people on the list of eligibles for that job. When the civil service commission receives this request, it sends to the agency the names of the three people highest on this list. Or, if the job to be filled has specialized requirements, the office sends the agency the names of the top three persons who meet these requirements from the general list.

The appointing officer makes a choice from among the three people whose names were sent to him. If the selected person accepts the appointment, the names of the others are put back on the list to be considered for future openings.

That is the rule in hiring from all kinds of eligible lists, whether they are for typist, carpenter, chemist, or something else. For every vacancy, the appointing officer has his choice of any one of the top three eligibles on the list. This explains why the person whose name is on top of the list sometimes does not get an appointment when some of the persons lower on the list do. If the appointing officer chooses the second or third eligible, the No. 1 eligible does not get a job at once, but stays on the list until he is appointed or the list is terminated.

X. HOW TO PASS THE INTERVIEW TEST

The examination for which you applied requires an oral interview test. You have already taken the written test and you are now being called for the interview test – the final part of the formal examination.

You may think that it is not possible to prepare for an interview test and that there are no procedures to follow during an interview. Our purpose is to point out some things you can do in advance that will help you and some good rules to follow and pitfalls to avoid while you are being interviewed.

What is an interview supposed to test?

The written examination is designed to test the technical knowledge and competence of the candidate; the oral is designed to evaluate intangible qualities, not readily measured otherwise, and to establish a list showing the relative fitness of each candidate – as measured against his competitors – for the position sought. Scoring is not on the basis of "right" and "wrong," but on a sliding scale of values ranging from "not passable" to "outstanding." As a matter of fact, it is possible to achieve a relatively low score without a single "incorrect" answer because of evident weakness in the qualities being measured.

Occasionally, an examination may consist entirely of an oral test – either an individual or a group oral. In such cases, information is sought concerning the technical knowledges and abilities of the candidate, since there has been no written examination for this purpose. More commonly, however, an oral test is used to supplement a written examination.

Who conducts interviews?

The composition of oral boards varies among different jurisdictions. In nearly all, a representative of the personnel department serves as chairman. One of the members of the board may be a representative of the department in which the candidate would work. In some cases, "outside experts" are used, and, frequently, a businessman or some other representative of the general public is asked to serve. Labor and management or other special groups may be represented. The aim is to secure the services of experts in the appropriate field.

However the board is composed, it is a good idea (and not at all improper or unethical) to ascertain in advance of the interview who the members are and what groups they represent. When you are introduced to them, you will have some idea of their backgrounds and interests, and at least you will not stutter and stammer over their names.

What should be done before the interview?

While knowledge about the board members is useful and takes some of the surprise element out of the interview, there is other preparation which is more substantive. It *is* possible to prepare for an oral interview – in several ways:

1) Keep a copy of your application and review it carefully before the interview

This may be the only document before the oral board, and the starting point of the interview. Know what education and experience you have listed there, and the sequence and dates of all of it. Sometimes the board will ask you to review the highlights of your experience for them; you should not have to hem and haw doing it.

2) Study the class specification and the examination announcement

Usually, the oral board has one or both of these to guide them. The qualities, characteristics or knowledges required by the position sought are stated in these documents. They offer valuable clues as to the nature of the oral interview. For example, if the job involves supervisory responsibilities, the announcement will usually indicate that knowledge of modern supervisory methods and the qualifications of the candidate as a supervisor will be tested. If so, you can expect such questions, frequently in the form of a hypothetical situation which you are expected to solve. NEVER go into an oral without knowledge of the duties and responsibilities of the job you seek.

3) Think through each qualification required

Try to visualize the kind of questions you would ask if you were a board member. How well could you answer them? Try especially to appraise your own knowledge and background in each area, *measured against the job sought*, and identify any areas in which you are weak. Be critical and realistic – do not flatter yourself.

4) Do some general reading in areas in which you feel you may be weak

For example, if the job involves supervision and your past experience has NOT, some general reading in supervisory methods and practices, particularly in the field of human relations, might be useful. Do NOT study agency procedures or detailed manuals. The oral board will be testing your understanding and capacity, not your memory.

5) Get a good night's sleep and watch your general health and mental attitude

You will want a clear head at the interview. Take care of a cold or any other minor ailment, and of course, no hangovers.

What should be done on the day of the interview?

Now comes the day of the interview itself. Give yourself plenty of time to get there. Plan to arrive somewhat ahead of the scheduled time, particularly if your appointment is in the fore part of the day. If a previous candidate fails to appear, the board might be ready for you a bit early. By early afternoon an oral board is almost invariably behind schedule if there are many candidates, and you may have to wait. Take along a book or magazine to read, or your application to review, but leave any extraneous material in the waiting room when you go in for your interview. In any event, relax and compose yourself.

The matter of dress is important. The board is forming impressions about you – from your experience, your manners, your attitude, and your appearance. Give your personal appearance careful attention. Dress your best, but not your flashiest. Choose conservative, appropriate clothing, and be sure it is immaculate. This is a business interview, and your appearance should indicate that you regard it as such. Besides, being well groomed and properly dressed will help boost your confidence.

Sooner or later, someone will call your name and escort you into the interview room. *This is it.* From here on you are on your own. It is too late for any more preparation. But remember, you asked for this opportunity to prove your fitness, and you are here because your request was granted.

What happens when you go in?

The usual sequence of events will be as follows: The clerk (who is often the board stenographer) will introduce you to the chairman of the oral board, who will introduce you to the other members of the board. Acknowledge the introductions before you sit down. Do not be surprised if you find a microphone facing you or a stenotypist sitting by. Oral interviews are usually recorded in the event of an appeal or other review.

Usually the chairman of the board will open the interview by reviewing the highlights of your education and work experience from your application – primarily for the benefit of the other members of the board, as well as to get the material into the record. Do not interrupt or comment unless there is an error or significant misinterpretation; if that is the case, do not hesitate. But do not quibble about insignificant matters. Also, he will usually ask you some question about your education, experience or your present job – partly to get you to start talking and to establish the interviewing "rapport." He may start the actual questioning, or turn it over to one of the other members. Frequently, each member undertakes the questioning on a particular area, one in which he is perhaps most competent, so you can expect each member to participate in the examination. Because time is limited, you may also expect some rather abrupt switches in the direction the questioning takes, so do not be upset by it. Normally, a board member will not pursue a single line of questioning unless he discovers a particular strength or weakness.

After each member has participated, the chairman will usually ask whether any member has any further questions, then will ask you if you have anything you wish to add. Unless you are expecting this question, it may floor you. Worse, it may start you off on an extended, extemporaneous speech. The board is not usually seeking more information. The question is principally to offer you a last opportunity to present further qualifications or to indicate that you have nothing to add. So, if you feel that a significant qualification or characteristic has been overlooked, it is proper to point it out in a sentence or so. Do not compliment the board on the thoroughness of their examination – they have been sketchy, and you know it. If you wish, merely say, "No thank you, I have nothing further to add." This is a point where you can "talk yourself out" of a good impression or fail to present an important bit of information. Remember, *you close the interview yourself.*

The chairman will then say, "That is all, Mr. _____, thank you." Do not be startled; the interview is over, and quicker than you think. Thank him, gather your belongings and take your leave. Save your sigh of relief for the other side of the door.

How to put your best foot forward

Throughout this entire process, you may feel that the board individually and collectively is trying to pierce your defenses, seek out your hidden weaknesses and embarrass and confuse you. Actually, this is not true. They are obliged to make an appraisal of your qualifications for the job you are seeking, and they want to see you in your best light. Remember, they must interview all candidates and a non-cooperative candidate may become a failure in spite of their best efforts to bring out his qualifications. Here are 15 suggestions that will help you:

1) Be natural – Keep your attitude confident, not cocky

If you are not confident that you can do the job, do not expect the board to be. Do not apologize for your weaknesses, try to bring out your strong points. The board is interested in a positive, not negative, presentation. Cockiness will antagonize any board member and make him wonder if you are covering up a weakness by a false show of strength.

2) Get comfortable, but don't lounge or sprawl

Sit erectly but not stiffly. A careless posture may lead the board to conclude that you are careless in other things, or at least that you are not impressed by the importance of the occasion. Either conclusion is natural, even if incorrect. Do not fuss with your clothing, a pencil or an ashtray. Your hands may occasionally be useful to emphasize a point; do not let them become a point of distraction.

3) Do not wisecrack or make small talk

This is a serious situation, and your attitude should show that you consider it as such. Further, the time of the board is limited – they do not want to waste it, and neither should you.

4) Do not exaggerate your experience or abilities

In the first place, from information in the application or other interviews and sources, the board may know more about you than you think. Secondly, you probably will not get away with it. An experienced board is rather adept at spotting such a situation, so do not take the chance.

5) If you know a board member, do not make a point of it, yet do not hide it

Certainly you are not fooling him, and probably not the other members of the board. Do not try to take advantage of your acquaintanceship – it will probably do you little good.

6) Do not dominate the interview

Let the board do that. They will give you the clues – do not assume that you have to do all the talking. Realize that the board has a number of questions to ask you, and do not try to take up all the interview time by showing off your extensive knowledge of the answer to the first one.

7) Be attentive

You only have 20 minutes or so, and you should keep your attention at its sharpest throughout. When a member is addressing a problem or question to you, give him your undivided attention. Address your reply principally to him, but do not exclude the other board members.

8) Do not interrupt

A board member may be stating a problem for you to analyze. He will ask you a question when the time comes. Let him state the problem, and wait for the question.

9) Make sure you understand the question

Do not try to answer until you are sure what the question is. If it is not clear, restate it in your own words or ask the board member to clarify it for you. However, do not haggle about minor elements.

10) Reply promptly but not hastily

A common entry on oral board rating sheets is "candidate responded readily," or "candidate hesitated in replies." Respond as promptly and quickly as you can, but do not jump to a hasty, ill-considered answer.

11) Do not be peremptory in your answers

A brief answer is proper – but do not fire your answer back. That is a losing game from your point of view. The board member can probably ask questions much faster than you can answer them.

12) Do not try to create the answer you think the board member wants

He is interested in what kind of mind you have and how it works – not in playing games. Furthermore, he can usually spot this practice and will actually grade you down on it.

13) Do not switch sides in your reply merely to agree with a board member

Frequently, a member will take a contrary position merely to draw you out and to see if you are willing and able to defend your point of view. Do not start a debate, yet do not surrender a good position. If a position is worth taking, it is worth defending.

14) Do not be afraid to admit an error in judgment if you are shown to be wrong

The board knows that you are forced to reply without any opportunity for careful consideration. Your answer may be demonstrably wrong. If so, admit it and get on with the interview.

15) Do not dwell at length on your present job

The opening question may relate to your present assignment. Answer the question but do not go into an extended discussion. You are being examined for a *new* job, not your present one. As a matter of fact, try to phrase ALL your answers in terms of the job for which you are being examined.

Basis of Rating

Probably you will forget most of these "do's" and "don'ts" when you walk into the oral interview room. Even remembering them all will not ensure you a passing grade. Perhaps you did not have the qualifications in the first place. But remembering them will help you to put your best foot forward, without treading on the toes of the board members.

Rumor and popular opinion to the contrary notwithstanding, an oral board wants you to make the best appearance possible. They know you are under pressure – but they also want to see how you respond to it as a guide to what your reaction would be under the pressures of the job you seek. They will be influenced by the degree of poise you display, the personal traits you show and the manner in which you respond.

ABOUT THIS BOOK

This book contains tests divided into Examination Sections. Go through each test, answering every question in the margin. We have also attached a sample answer sheet at the back of the book that can be removed and used. At the end of each test look at the answer key and check your answers. On the ones you got wrong, look at the right answer choice and learn. Do not fill in the answers first. Do not memorize the questions and answers, but understand the answer and principles involved. On your test, the questions will likely be different from the samples. Questions are changed and new ones added. If you understand these past questions you should have success with any changes that arise. Tests may consist of several types of questions. We have additional books on each subject should more study be advisable or necessary for you. Finally, the more you study, the better prepared you will be. This book is intended to be the last thing you study before you walk into the examination room. Prior study of relevant texts is also recommended. NLC publishes some of these in our Fundamental Series. Knowledge and good sense are important factors in passing your exam. Good luck also helps. So now study this Passbook, absorb the material contained within and take that knowledge into the examination. Then do your best to pass that exam.

EXAMINATION SECTION

EXAMINATION SECTION
TEST 1

DIRECTIONS: Each question or incomplete statement is followed by several suggested answers or completions. Select the one that BEST answers the question or completes the statement. *PRINT THE LETTER OF THE CORRECT ANSWER IN THE SPACE AT THE RIGHT.*

Questions 1-4.

DIRECTIONS: Questions 1 through 4 are to be answered using only the information in the following passage.

Planning for storage layout in terms of the supplies to be stored involves the intelligent and realistic application of a stockman's basic resources - space. The main objective of storage planning is the maximum use of available space. The planning and layout of space are dependent upon the types of supplies expected to be stored, and certain characteristics must be considered. Some supplies must be protected from dampness, extreme changes of temperature, and other such conditions. Iron and steel products rust quickly at high temperatures with high humidity. High temperatures also cause some plastics to melt and change shape, while extreme dampness can cause paper to mildew and wood to warp. Hazardous articles, including flammable items like paint and rubber cement, should be stored separated from each other and from other types of supplies.

Extremes in characteristics such as size, shape, and weight need to be considered in laying out space. Large, awkward containers and unusually heavy items generally should be stored near doors with aisles leading directly to them and/or shipping and receiving facilities. Light and fragile items cannot be stacked to a height which would cause crushing or other damage to containers and contents. Fast-moving articles should be stored in locations from which they can be handled quickly and efficiently.

1. It is MOST important to store articles like paints and rubber cement in areas where   1.____
    A. they can be protected from theft
    B. shipping and receiving doors are easily accessible
    C. they can be isolated from other supplies
    D. boxes containing them can be stacked as high as possible

2. Storage locations from which items can be selected and issued quickly are recommended for supplies classified as   2.____
    A. fragile
    B. fast-moving
    C. under-sized
    D. flammable

3. In order to prevent supplies made of iron from rusting, they should be stored in areas with _____ humidity and _____ temperature.   3.____
    A. low; high
    B. low; low
    C. high; high
    D. high; low

4. Which of the following characteristics is NOT considered in the above passage on storage planning and layout?   4.____
    The _____ of the item to be stored.
    A. size   B. quantity   C. weight   D. shape

Questions 5-12.

DIRECTIONS: Each of Questions 5 through 12 consists of a word in capitals followed by four suggested meanings of the word. For each question, choose the meaning which you think is BEST and print the letter of the correct answer in the space at the right.

5. CATALOG 5.___
   A. to list   B. to rate   C. to print   D. to price

6. DURABLE 6.___
   A. smooth   B. sticky   C. lasting   D. feeling

7. MUTUAL 7.___
   A. silent   B. shared   C. changing   D. broken

8. REJECT 8.___
   A. rewrite   B. refuse   C. release   D. regret

9. OBSTRUCT 9.___
   A. teach   B. darken   C. block   D. resist

10. CORRODE 10.___
   A. melt   B. rust   C. burn   D. warp

11. EXCESS 11.___
   A. surplus   B. storage   C. spacing   D. survey

12. FLEXIBLE 12.___
   A. neatly folded   B. easily broken
   C. easily bent   D. neatly piled

Questions 13-16.

DIRECTIONS: Questions 13 through 16 are to be answered using ONLY the information in the following passage.

   The "active stock" portion of the inventory is that portion which is kept for the purpose of satisfying the shop's expected requirements of that material. It is directly related to the "order quantity." The "order quantity" is found by determining the expected annual requirements of the shop and dividing this by the number of orders for this merchandise which will be placed during the year. The most economical number of orders is usually found by considering the cost of ordering and storing inventory.

   The "safety stock" portion of the inventory is that portion which is created to take care of above-average or unexpected demands on the inventory. This portion is directly related to the point at which the order is placed. The amount of safety stock is not determined by com-

paring order costs and carrying costs, but on the need for protection against stock shortages for each stock item under consideration. Some stock items will need more safety stock than others, depending upon how much difference there has been in the past between the expected usage of material and the actual amount needed and used for any given time period, plus the reliability of the suppliers' delivery and of the order lead-time. If the expected usage of an item has always been 100% accurately predicted, then theoretically there would be no need for "safety stock."

13. According to the above passage, the *active stock* inventory is that portion of the inventory which is

    A. used most frequently by management
    B. ordered on a regular basis, such as every month
    C. expected to meet the organization's anticipated inventory needs
    D. needed to protect against shortages in very active inventory items

14. According to the above passage, what factors must be considered to determine the order quantity for any active stock item?

    A. Anticipated requirements, ordering cost, and cost of storing inventory
    B. Order lead-time and delivery service
    C. Variety of stock items ordered in the previous year
    D. The largest quantity ever ordered

15. Maintaining a safety stock portion of the inventory is

    A. *good,* because it provides for unexpected demands on the inventory
    B. *good,* because it makes the inventory more valuable than it actually is
    C. *poor,* because it provides unnecessary work for stockmen since the Inventory is rarely used
    D. *poor,* because it makes storage areas overcrowded and unsafe

16. The above passage indicates that 100 percent accuracy in forecasting future activity will eliminate the need for

    A. reliable deliveries
    B. active stock
    C. safety stock
    D. deviation in total order quantity

17. At the start of a certain month, you have 185 jars of glue in stock. During that month, you fill the following orders: 3 orders for 12 jars each, 2 orders for 10 jars each, 2 orders for 8 jars each, one order for 9 jars, one order for 20 jars, and one order for 24 jars.
    If you received no shipments of glue during that month, the number of jars of glue you will have on hand at the end of the month is

    A. 60   B. 77   C. 102   D. 125

18. Assume that you are ordering merchandise from a vendor who gives a discount of 10%, plus an additional 2% for payment within 30 days.
    If, on October 21st, you order merchandise which has a catalogue value of $714, and the bill is paid by November 10th, the net amount of the payment should be MOST NEARLY

    A. $628.32   B. $629.95   C. $630.74   D. $632.60

19. Suppose that there are 293 people in your shop and 11% of them are women. The number of men in your shop is

    A. 261   B. 263   C. 269   D. 271

20. In March, Department Z made an overpayment of $34.26 to the Superior Fuel Oil Company. This amount was credited to the Department's account. In April, the fuel bill amounted to $378.12.
    Considering the credit on the Department's account, the payment that should be remitted for the April fuel bill is

    A. $343.86   B. $343.96   C. $344.86   D. $344.96

21. A certain agency ordered and used 1,020 one-pound balls of twine last year at a total cost of $357.
    If the price per ball of twine remained constant throughout the year, the cost of each one-pound ball was

    A. 25¢   B. 30¢   C. 35¢   D. 40¢

22. You place an order at the Abbey Office Supply Company for three of each of the following items: metal desk at $129 each; chair at $65 each; desk lamp at $24 each.
    If this supply company gives a 15% discount on all orders totaling $500 or more, the net price of this order is

    A. $567.90   B. $555.90   C. $484.20   D. $479.20

23. Suppose that there are 27 people in your department and your boss tells you that he is putting on an extra laborer and two mechanics.
    The percent of the increase in personnel for your department would be MOST NEARLY

    A. 8%   B. 9%   C. 10%   D. 11%

Questions 24-29.

DIRECTIONS:

CODE TABLE

Code Letter	b	d	f	a	g	s	z	w	h	u
Code Number	1	2	3	4	5	6	7	8	9	0

In the Code Table above, each code letter has a corresponding code number directly beneath it.

Each of Questions 24 through 29 contains three sets of code letters and code numbers. In each set, the code numbers should correspond with the code letters as given in the table, but there is a coding error in some of the sets. Examine the sets in each question carefully.

Mark your answer:
  A if there is a coding error in only ONE of the sets in the question;
  B if there is a coding error in any TWO of the sets in the question;
  C if there is a coding error in all THREE sets in the question;
  D if there is a coding error in NONE of the sets in the question.

SAMPLE QUESTION:

  fgzduwaf - 35720843
  uabsdgfw - 04262538
  hhfaudgs - 99340257

In the sample question above, the first set is right because each code number matches the code letter as in the Code Table. In the second set, the corresponding number for the code letter b is wrong because it should be 1 instead of 2. In the third set, the corresponding number for the last code letter s is wrong because it should be 6 instead of 7. Since there is an error in two of the sets, the answer to the above sample question is B.

24. fsbughwz - 36104987   24._____
     zwubgasz - 78025467
     ghgufddb - 59583221

25. hafgdaas - 94351446   25._____
     ddsfabsd - 22734162
     wgdbssgf - 85216553

26. abfbssbd - 41316712   26._____
     ghzfaubs - 59734017
     sdbzfwza - 62173874

27. whfbdzag - 89412745   27._____
     daaszuub - 24467001
     uzhfwssd - 07936623

28. zbadgbuh - 71425109   28._____
     dzadbbsz - 27421167
     gazhwaff - 54798433

29. fbfuadsh - 31304265   29._____
     gzfuwzsb - 57300671
     bashhgag - 14699535

Questions 30-35.

DIRECTIONS: Questions 30 through 35 are to be answered on the basis of the information in the Weekly Requisition Form below.

WEEKLY REQUISITION FORM

Storehouse 17	Date 7.17	Dept. Code 809	Dept. Budget Code 13942	Dept. Requisition No. 1029	
Deliver to: Requisition Dept. Atlantic Hospital			Unit and/or Division Kitchen	Address 66 W. Highland Blvd.	
Storehouse Item Code	Description Incl. Size, Number or Measurements		Unit of Issue	No. Units Requested	Unit Price	Tot. Cost
895	Chocolate Syrup #10 can		case	5	7.35	
1926	Mayonnaise 1 gal. jar		case	2	6.73	13.46
1945	Black pepper, ground 1.lb. can		lb	3		1.89
1976	34 fresh eggs			7	.41	2.87
220	Pineapple, crushed #10 can		case	4	5.89	23.56
5395	Straws 8 1/2" long 500 to box		box	12	.47	5.64
452	Applesauce 4 1/2 oz. jar 24/case		case		1.65	6.60
Requested By John Smith	Title Shop Clerk	Material Issued By _____ Date _____		Material Received By Signed _____ Date _____		
Approved By _____	Supervisor	Total No. Pieces _____		Total No. Pieces _____		

30. What is the total cost of the chocolate syrup order described in the requisition form above?

    A. $36.75   B. $34.35   C. $31.65   D. $30.15

31. The week of 7/24, the price of a gallon jar of mayonnaise increased by 4 cents. If there are 6 gallon jars of mayonnaise per case, how much is the total cost of the mayonnaise order for the week of 7/24, if the order quantity is the same as the previous week?

    A. $6.97   B. $7.21   C. $13.68   D. $13.94

32. What is the unit price for ground black pepper as described in the requisition form above?

    A. 36¢   B. 43¢   C. 57¢   D. 63¢

33. Based on the information provided in the requisition form above, what is the correct unit of issue for fresh eggs?

    A. Each   B. Container   C. Dozen   D. Case

34. There are 6 #10 cans of crushed pineapple per case. Based on the information in the requisition form above, how many #10 cans of pineapple are being ordered?

    A. 16   B. 20   C. 24   D. 30

35. Each week the cook at Atlantic Hospital uses 84 4 1/2 ounce jars of applesauce. Based on the requisition for the week of 7/17, how many cases must be ordered to fill the need for the following week (7/24) in order to avoid storing an excess supply of applesauce? (Assume that there was no excess from the week previous to 7/17.)

    A. 1   B. 2   C. 3   D. 4

36. Suppose that the shop in which you worked received 421 pieces of mail in one month, of which 64 were requests for information.
    The percent of letters which were requests for information is MOST NEARLY

    A. 13.2%   B. 15.2%   C. 15.5%   D. 16.1%

37. The following is the year's stock issue record of cans of oil distributed for use in Agency Y: January - 107; February - 94; March - 113; April - 118; May - 122; June - 87; July - 89; August - 98; September - 110; October - 101; November - 105; December - 106.
    The monthly average of cans of oil distributed is MOST NEARLY

    A. 100   B. 102   C. 104   D. 106

38. Two trucks, A and B, are carrying stock from a warehouse to the shop. The weight of the truck alone is the tare; the weight of the loaded truck is the gross weight. Truck A has a tare of 4,637 pounds, and a gross weight of 6,955 pounds. Truck B has a tare of 4,489 pounds, and a gross weight of 6,723 pounds.
    What is the total weight of the loads of both trucks?
    _____ pounds.

    A. 3,452   B. 3,564   C. 4,552   D. 4,653

39. A stock carton measures 24" long, 18" wide, and 24" high. What is the maximum number of boxes measuring 4 1/2" long, 3" wide, and 3" high that can be packed inside the carton?

    A. 135   B. 256   C. 405   D. 432

40. If a ream of paper weighs 11 ounces, 36 reams of paper will weigh _____ pounds, _____ ounces.

    A. 22; 8   B. 24; 12   C. 33; 0   D. 39; 6

KEY (CORRECT ANSWERS)

1.	C	11.	A	21.	C	31.	D
2.	B	12.	C	22.	B	32.	D
3.	B	13.	C	23.	D	33.	C
4.	B	14.	A	24.	C	34.	C
5.	A	15.	A	25.	C	35.	C
6.	C	16.	C	26.	B	36.	B
7.	B	17.	A	27.	B	37.	C
8.	B	18.	A	28.	D	38.	C
9.	C	19.	A	29.	C	39.	B
10.	B	20.	A	30.	A	40.	B

TEST 2

DIRECTIONS: Each question or incomplete statement is followed by several suggested answers or completions. Select the one that BEST answers the question or completes the statement. *PRINT THE LETTER OF THE CORRECT ANSWER IN THE SPACE AT THE RIGHT.*

Questions 1-6.

DIRECTIONS: Questions 1 through 6 are to be answered on the basis of the information below.

A certain shop keeps an informational card file for all suppliers and merchandise. On each card is the supplier's name, the contract number for the merchandise he supplies, and a delivery date for the merchandise. In this filing system, the supplier's name is filed alphabetically, the contract number for the merchandise is filed numerically, and the delivery date is filed chronologically.

In Questions 1 through 6, there are five notations numbered 1 through 5 shown in Column I. Each notation is made up of a supplier's name, a contract number, and a date and is to be filed according to the following rules:

First: File in alphabetical order
Second: When two or more notations have the same supplier, file according to the contract number in numerical order beginning with the lowest number
Third: When two or more notations have the same supplier and contract number, file according to the date beginning with the earliest date

In Column II, the numbers 1 through 5 are arranged in four ways to show different possible orders in which the merchandise information might be filed. Pick the answer (A, B, C, or D) in Column II in which the notations are arranged according to the above filing rules.

SAMPLE QUESTION:

Column I
1. Cluney (4865) 6/17/72
2. Roster (2466) 5/10/71
3. Altool (7114) 10/15/72
4. Cluney (5276) 12/18/71
5. Cluney (4865) 4/8/72

Column II
A. 2, 3, 4, 1, 5
B. 2, 5, 1, 3, 4
C. 3, 2, 1, 4, 5
D. 3, 5, 1, 4, 2

The correct way to file the notations is:
(3) Altool (7114) 10/15/72
(5) Cluney (4865) 4/8/72
(1) Cluney (4865) 6/17/72
(4) Cluney (5276) 12/18/71
(2) Roster (2466) 5/10/71

Since the correct filing order is 3, 5, 1, 4, 2, the answer to the sample question is D.

	Column I		Column II	
1.	1. Fenten (38511) 1/4/73 2. Meadowlane (5020) 11/1/72 3. Whitehall (36142) 6/22/72 4. Clinton (4141) 5/26/71 5. Mester (8006) 4/20/71	A. B. C. D.	3, 5, 2, 1, 4 4, 1, 2, 5, 3 4, 2, 5, 3, 1 5, 4, 3, 1, 2	1.__
2.	1. Harvard (2286) 2/19/70 2. Parker (1781) 4/12/72 3. Lenson (9044) 6/6/72 4. Brothers (38380) 10/11/72 5. Parker (41400) 12/20/70	A. B. C. D.	2, 4, 3, 1, 5 2, 1, 3, 4, 5 4, 1, 3, 2, 5 5, 2, 3, 1, 4	2.__
3.	1. Newtone (3197) 8/22/70 2. Merritt (4071) 8/8/72 3. Writebest (60666) 4/7/71 4. Maltons (34380) 3/30/72 5. Merrit (4071) 7/16/71	A. B. C. D.	1, 4, 2, 5, 3 4, 2, 1, 5, 3 4, 5, 2, 1, 3 5, 2, 4, 3, 1	3.__
4.	1. Weinburt (45514) 6/4/71 2. Owntye (35860) 10/4/72 3. Weinburt (45515) 2/1/72 4. Fasttex (7677) 11/10/71 5. Owntye (4574) 7/17/72	A. B. C. D.	4, 5, 2, 1, 3 4, 2, 5, 3, 1 4, 2, 5, 1, 3 4, 5, 2, 3, 1	4.__
5.	1. Premier (1003) 7/29/70 2. Phylson (0031) 5/5/72 3. Lathen (3328) 10/3/71 4. Harper (8046) 8/18/72 5. Lathen (3328) 12/1/72	A. B. C. D.	2, 1, 4, 3, 5 3, 5, 4, 1, 2 4, 1, 2, 3, 5 4, 3, 5, 2, 1	5.__
6.	1. Repper (46071) 10/14/72 2. Destex (77271) 8/27/72 3. Clawson (30736) 7/28/71 4. Destex (27207) 8/17/71 5. Destex (77271) 4/14/71	A. B. C. D.	3, 2, 4, 5, 1 3, 4, 2, 5, 1 3, 4, 5, 2, 1 3, 5, 4, 2, 1	6.__

7. Assume that a clerk is asked to prepare a special report which he has not prepared before. He decides to make a written outline of the report before writing it in full. This decision by the clerk is

   A. *good,* mainly because it helps the writer to organize his thoughts and decide what will go into the report
   B. *good,* mainly because it clearly shows the number of topics, number of pages, and the length of the report
   C. *poor,* mainly because it wastes the time of the writer since he will have to write the full report anyway
   D. *poor,* mainly because it confines the writer to those areas listed in the outline

7.__

8. Assume that a clerk in the water resources central shop is asked to prepare an important report, giving the location and condition of various fire hydrants in the city. One of the hydrants in question is broken and is spewing rusty water in the street, creating a flooded condition in the area. The clerk reports that the hydrant is broken but does not report the escaping water or the flood.
Of the following, the BEST evaluation of the clerk's decision about what to report is that it is basically

8._____

A. *correct,* chiefly because a lengthy report would contain irrelevant information
B. *correct,* chiefly because a more detailed description of a hydrant should be made by a fireman, not a clerk
C. *incorrect,* chiefly because the clerk's assignment was to describe the condition of the hydrant and he should give a full explanation
D. *incorrect,* chiefly because the clerk should include as much information as possible in his report whether or not it is relevant

Questions 9-14.

DIRECTIONS: Questions 9 through 14 are to be answered ONLY on the information contained in the following chart, which shows the number of requisitions filled by Storeroom A during each month of the year.

NUMBER OF REQUISITIONS HANDLED EACH MONTH
DURING THE YEAR BY STOREROOM A

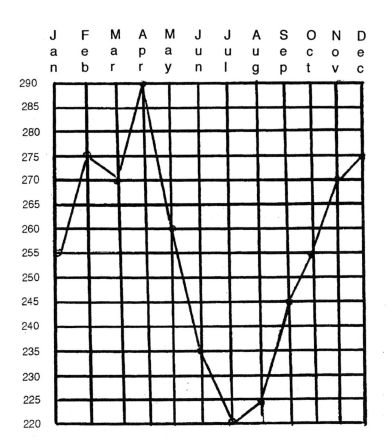

9. According to the above chart, the average number of requisitions handled per month by Storeroom A during the first six months of the year is MOST NEARLY

   A. 250 B. 260 C. 270 D. 280

10. It is expected that the number of requisitions Storeroom A will handle next year will be 10 percent more than it handled this year.
    The number of requisitions Storeroom A is expected to handle next year will MOST likely be

    A. 2,763 B. 3,070 C. 3,382 D. 3,440

11. The month during which the number of requisitions handled showed the GREATEST decrease from the previous month was

    A. April B. May C. June D. July

12. During May there were 3 clerks assigned to Storeroom A. One man went on vacation for the month of June and was not replaced.
    The number of additional orders handled by each man working in June over the number of orders handled per man in May was MOST NEARLY

    A. 20 B. 27 C. 32 D. 36

13. During June, July, and August, 8 percent of the requisitions handled were rush orders.
    The number of rush orders handled during these three months is MOST NEARLY

    A. 55 B. 60 C. 65 D. 70

14. During November, there were three clerks assigned to Storeroom A.
    If one handled 95 requisitions and another handled 85 requisitions, the number of requisitions handled by the third clerk was

    A. 70 B. 80 C. 90 D. 100

15. In which of the following cases would it be MOST desirable to repack the contents of a carton which was just received in a shipment?

    A. You expect to keep the packed carton in the shop for several months.
    B. The carton is not strong enough to support the weight of another carton you want to put on top of it.
    C. You intend to ship the carton to another location, with a different address.
    D. You want to check the contents of the carton to be sure that you received the correct shipment.

16. The daily reports regarding subway cars that are out of service must be prepared in great detail. All known information about each of the cars must be included in the report, even if such information is lengthy and not related to the reason the car is out of service.
    Of the following, the MOST accurate evaluation of this statement is that it is basically

    A. *correct*, mainly because it is important to supply the reader with background information about the topic of the report
    B. *correct*, mainly because detailed reports make a more favorable impression upon the reader

C. *incorrect*, mainly because a good report should be as brief as possible and contain only relevant information
D. *incorrect*, mainly because background information about each car should be supplied in a separate report

Questions 17-22.

DIRECTIONS: Questions 17 through 22 are to be answered ONLY on the basis of the information in the chart below.

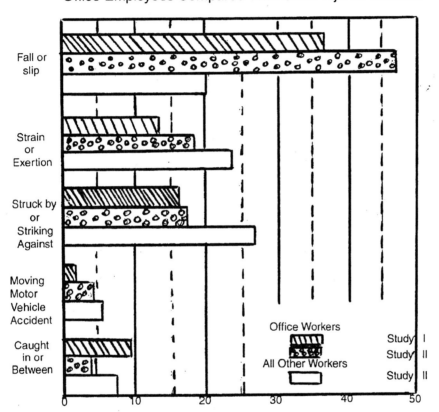

The above chart shows the results of two studies concerning injuries to office workers. Study I was done only for office workers. The results are represented by ▨, Study II compared injuries to office workers with injuries to all other workers. In Study II, office workers are represented by ▦; all other workers by ▢

17. In Study II, in which category of accident was there a 5% difference between the percentage of Office Workers injured and the percentage of All Other Workers injured? 17._____

    A. Strain or Exertion
    B. Struck by or Striking Against
    C. Moving Motor Vehicle Accident
    D. Caught In or Between

18. In which category of accident is the average percentage of all Office Workers injured closest to the percentage of injuries for All Other Workers?

    A. Fall or Slip
    B. Strain or Exertion
    C. Struck By or Striking Against
    D. Caught In or Between

19. In which category is the percentage of All Other Workers injured MOST NEARLY one-half of the average percentage for all Office Workers injured?

    A. Fall or Slip
    B. Strain or Exertion
    C. Struck By or Striking Against
    D. Moving Motor Vehicle Accident

20. In which category of injuries is the percentage of injured Office Workers in Study I shown to be closest to the percentage of injured Office Workers in Study II?

    A. Strain or Exertion
    B. Struck By or Striking Against
    C. Moving Motor Vehicle Accident
    D. Caught In or Between

21. The percentage of Office Workers shown injured in Study II for the category of accident Strain or Exertion is BEST described as being more than _____ less than _____ .

    A. 5%; 10%   B. 10%; 15%   C. 15%; 20%   D. 20%; 24%

22. The largest percentage of injuries shown on the above chart for the group All Other Workers is BEST described as being MOST NEARLY

    A. 18%   B. 21%   C. 24%   D. 27%

23. Suppose that you have trained a new clerk to assist you in handling the stockroom. A few weeks later, you put him in charge of inventory control for one-half of the stockroom. When making a periodic check of the way he is keeping his records, you find quite a difference between supplies actually on hand and the amount shown to be in stock on the inventory record cards.
    Of the following, the BEST action to take in this situation is to

    A. report the clerk to your supervisor because he is not keeping the records properly
    B. tell the clerk that you will order an additional supply of the items to cover the difference
    C. review the inventory control procedure with the clerk in order to locate the source of the error
    D. advise the clerk that he is not suited for this job and that you will recommend that he be transferred

24. You are the clerk in charge of the time cards on which the men in the shop sign in in the mornings and sign out in the afternoons. Suppose that one day a co-worker with whom you are especially friendly asks you to let him sign 15 minutes before the others so that he can get a seat on the subway.
    Of the following, which is the MOST desirable action to take?

A. Go on and let your friend sign out; no one will know about it except the two of you
B. Tell your friend you'll let him sign out this first time, but warn him not to ask again
C. Tell your friend you are going to report him to your supervisor and to his, so he will not try anything like this again
D. Explain to your friend that this is a violation of the rules and that, even though you're friends, you cannot grant his request

25. Suppose that one of the road crew working in a shop receives a great many personal phone calls and constantly requests the clerk to take detailed messages for him. Taking these messages is beginning to take up a lot of the clerk's time.
The BEST thing for the clerk to do under the circumstances is to

    A. tell the man's supervisor that he should put a stop to his men receiving so many personal phone calls
    B. purposely omit or confuse some messages so the worker will stop requesting that he take them
    C. explain to the worker that he cannot spend so much time taking messages because it is interfering with his work
    D. continue to take the messages, but write a report to the worker's supervisor complaining about the phone calls

25.____

26. For a six-month period including the previous months, 6 additional mechanics are assigned to work in a shop for a special assignment. The clerk must prepare a vacation schedule for all the men in the shop based on the men's requests and their seniority in the department. Several of the 12 *regulars* in the shop believe they should be given priority, and ask the clerk to do so, even though some of the other men have greater seniority.
Under the circumstances, the clerk should

    A. immediately report the *regulars* to their supervisor for trying to break the rules
    B. tell them that, since all the men are assigned to the shop, he must make up the schedule as if they were all *regulars*
    C. try to satisfy the *regulars* since they will be around as co-workers after the other 6 men leave
    D. tell the new men that some of the *regulars* are trying to make trouble for them

26.____

27. Assume that you receive a written complaint from an irate vendor shortly after your supervisor has begun his vacation. The supervisor is not expected back for several weeks. The complaint is complex, and you are uncertain about how to reply to it.
Of the following, the BEST course of action for you to take in this situation is to

    A. answer the vendor's complaint as well as you can
    B. assign a clerk in your shop to reply to the vendor's complaint
    C. wait until your supervisor returns from vacation
    D. write to the vendor to tell him that the complaint has been received and that your office is looking into it

27.____

28. Suppose that you are a clerk in a transit authority repair shop. A member of the public has called the transit authority to complain about poor ventilation in a subway car, and the call has been transferred to your office. The man demands to speak to the foreman, who is gone for the day to attend a meeting. The man becomes increasingly angry and abusive when you tell him the foreman has gone.
Under the circumstances, the BEST thing for you to do is to

28.____

A. tell the man that if he continues to yell at you you will hang up
B. try to calm the man down and then tell him you will record his complaint and report it to the foreman
C. speak to the man as loudly and rudely as he is speaking to you until he calms down
D. hang up the telephone since the man is not rational and there is no point in talking to him

29. You and a co-worker are both asked by your supervisor to work on a job that requires two men working full-time to complete it on time. You find that your co-worker is *goofing off* and not doing his share of the work.
Of the following, the FIRST thing you should do is to

A. try to do enough work for two of you, so the job will be finished on time
B. begin to goof off also, so your co-worker will not think he can take advantage of you
C. tell your co-worker that you think he is not doing his share, and that you will have to go to the supervisor if he doesn't straighten out
D. report your co-worker to your supervisor, and tell the supervisor you refuse to continue unless he assigns someone else to work with you

Questions 30-33.

DIRECTIONS: Questions 30 through 33 are to be answered on the basis of the information in the report below.

To: Chief, Division X
From: Mrs. Helen Jones, Clerk
Subject: Accident Involving Two Employees, Mr. John Smith and Mr. Robert Brown

On February 15, Mr. Smith and Mr. Brown were both injured in an accident occurring in the shop at 10 Long Road. No one was in the area of the accident other than Mr. Smith and Mr. Brown. Both of these employees described the following circumstances:

1. Mr. Brown saw the largest tool on the wall begin to fall from where it was hanging and ran up to push Mr. Smith out of the way and to prevent the tool from falling, if possible.
2. Mr. Smith was standing near the wall under some tools which were hanging on nails in the wall.
3. Mr. Brown was standing a few steps from the wall.
4. Mr. Brown stepped toward Mr. Smith, who was on the floor and away from the falling tool. He tripped and fell over a piece of equipment on the floor.
5. Mr. Brown pushed Mr. Smith who slipped on some grease on the floor and fell to the side, out of the way of the falling tool.
6. Mr. Brown tried to avoid Mr. Smith as he fell. In so doing, he fell against some pipes which were leaning against the wall. The pipes fell on both Mr. Brown and Mr. Smith.

Mr. Smith and Mr. Brown were both badly bruised and shaken. They were sent to the General Hospital to determine if any bones were broken. The office was later notified that neither employee was seriously hurt.

Since the accident, matters relating to safety and accident prevention around the shop have occupied the staff. There have been a number of complaints about the location of tools and equipment. Several employees are reluctant to work in the shop unless conditions are improved. Please advise as to the best way to handle this situation.

30. The one of the following which it is MOST important to add to the above memorandum is   30.____

    A. a signature line
    B. a transmittal note
    C. the date of the memo
    D. the initials of the typist

31. The MOST logical order in which to list the circumstances relative to the accident is   31.____

    A. as shown (1, 2, 3, 4, 5, 6)
    B. 2, 3, 1, 5, 4, 6
    C. 1, 5, 4, 6, 3, 2
    D. 3, 2, 4, 6, 1, 5

32. The one of the following which does NOT properly belong with the rest of the memorandum is   32.____

    A. the first section of paragraph 1
    B. the list of circumstances
    C. paragraph 2
    D. paragraph 3

33. According to the information in the memorandum, the BEST description of the subject is   33.____

    A. effect of accident on work output of the division
    B. description of accident involving Mr. Smith and Mr. Brown
    C. recommendations on how to avoid future accidents
    D. safety and accident control in the shop

34. The items of stock which should usually be issued FIRST are those which   34.____

    A. are of best quality
    B. are of poorest quality
    C. have been longest in the storeroom
    D. are not being stored any more

35. If all the new stock of a certain item will not fit on the shelf where the old stock is stored, it would usually be BEST to   35.____

    A. store some of the stock in a new location
    B. store the excess stock in the aisle near the shelf
    C. keep the new stock in the receiving area until the old stock is issued
    D. move all the stock to a new location

36. The MAJOR purpose of maintaining an adequate inventory is to

    A. prevent supply shortages
    B. reduce waste of storage space
    C. increase the dollar value of the organization
    D. provide enough jobs for stockmen

37. The term *This Side Up* is MOST appropriate on a carton containing

    A. canned food   B. boxes of paper clips
    C. clothing   D. a typewriter

38. Storeroom records are essential in order to have a supply of each stock item always available.
    What information is it NOT necessary to include in storeroom records?

    A. When to reorder stock items
    B. Required delivery time
    C. Means of transportation of delivery
    D. Sources of stock supply

39. Assume that you usually order a new supply of tires for your agency's fleet of trucks every 6 months. Just before you place an order, you find out that there is a 10% increase expected in the price of tires during the next 3 months.
    Of the following, the BEST action for you to take FIRST is to

    A. automatically order a double supply of tires before the prices are increased in order to save the 10%
    B. ignore the expected price increase because it is only expected, not definite
    C. determine what the storage and other costs for an extra order of tires will be and compare it with the cost of a 10% price increase
    D. wait until the new prices go into effect because the more expensive tires will probably be better quality

40. Assume that your supervisor asks you to do a certain job of unpacking cartons. He tells you how to do it, but you believe there is a better, faster way.
    The MOST advisable course of action for you to take is to

    A. follow your supervisor's orders and unpack the cartons his way, without comment
    B. unpack the cartons your way and then show your supervisor the result
    C. ask your co-workers which way they think is better, and do the job that way
    D. explain your way to your supervisor and then ask him which method you should use

KEY (CORRECT ANSWERS)

1.	B	11.	B	21.	C	31.	B
2.	C	12.	C	22.	D	32.	D
3.	C	13.	A	23.	C	33.	B
4.	A	14.	C	24.	D	34.	C
5.	D	15.	B	25.	C	35.	A
6.	C	16.	C	26.	B	36.	A
7.	A	17.	A	27.	D	37.	D
8.	C	18.	D	28.	B	38.	C
9.	B	19.	A	29.	C	39.	C
10.	C	20.	B	30.	C	40.	D

EXAMINATION SECTION
TEST 1

DIRECTIONS: Each question or incomplete statement is followed by several suggested answers or completions. Select the one that BEST answers the question or completes the statement. *PRINT THE LETTER OF THE CORRECT ANSWER IN THE SPACE AT THE RIGHT.*

1. A shop clerk is notified that only 75 bolts can be supplied by Vendor A. If this represents 12.5% of the total requisition, then how many bolts were *originally* ordered?

    A. 125   B. 600   C. 700   D. 900

2. An enclosed square-shaped storage area with sides of 16 feet each has a safe-load capacity of 250 pounds per square foot.
   The MAXIMUM evenly distributed weight that can be stored in this area is _____ lbs.

    A. 1,056   B. 4,000   C. 64,000   D. 102,400

3. A clerical employee has completed 70 progress reports the first week, 87 the second week, and 80 the third week. Assuming a 4-week month, how many progress reports must the clerk complete in the fourth week in order to attain an average of 85 progress reports per week for the month?

    A. 93   B. 103   C. 113   D. 133

4. On the first of the month, Shop X received a delivery of 150 gallons of lubricating oil. During the month, the following amounts of oil were used on lubricating work each week: 30 quarts, 36 quarts, 20 quarts, and 48 quarts. The amount of lubricating oil *remaining* at the end of the month was _____ gallons.

    A. 4   B. 33.5   C. 41.5   D. 116.5

5. For working a 35-hour week, Employee A earns a gross amount of $480.90. For each hour that Employee A works over 40 hours a week, he is entitled to 1 1/2 times his hourly wage rate.
   If Employee A worked 9 hours on Monday, 8 hours on Tuesday, 9 hours 30 minutes on Wednesday, 9 hours 15 minutes on Thursday, and 9 hours 15 minutes on Friday, what should his *gross* salary be for that week?

    A. $618.30   B. $632.04   C. $652.65   D. $687.00

6. An enclosed cube-shaped storage bay has dimensions of 12 feet by 12 feet by 12 feet. Standard procedure requires that there be at least 1 foot of space between the walls, the ceiling, and the stored items.
   What is the MAXIMUM number of cube-shaped boxes with length, width, and height of 1 foot each that can be stored on 1-foot high pallets in this bay?

    A. 1,000   B. 1,331   C. 1,452   D. 1,728

7. Assume that two ceilings are to be painted. One ceiling measures 30 feet by 15 feet and the second 45 feet by 60 feet.
   If one quart of paint will cover 60 square feet of ceiling, *approximately* how much paint will be required to paint the two ceilings? _____ gallons.

A. 6   B. 10   C. 13   D. 18

8. In last year's budget, $7,500 was spent for office supplies. Of this amount, 60% was spent for paper supplies. If the price of paper has risen 20% over last year's price, then the amount that will be spent this year on paper supplies, assuming the same quantity will be purchased, will be

   A. $3,600   B. $5,200   C. $5,400   D. $6,000

8.___

Questions 9-13.

DIRECTIONS: Questions 9 through 13 are to be answered on the basis of the following information.

A certain shop keeps an informational card file on all suppliers and merchandise. On each card is the supplier's name, the contrast number for the merchandise he supplies, and a delivery date for the merchandise. In this filing system, the supplier's name is filed alphabetically, the contract number for the merchandise is filed numerically, and the delivery date is filed chronologically.

In Questions 9 through 13, there are five notations numbered 1 through 5 shown in Column I. Each notation is made up of a supplier's name, a contract number, and a date which is to be filed according to the following rules:

   First: File in alphabetical order
   Second: When two or more notations have the same supplier,
            file according to the contract number in numerical
            order beginning with the lowest number
   Third: When two or more notations have the same supplier
            and contract number, file according to the date
            beginning with the earliest date.

In Column II, the numbers 1 through 5 are arranged in four ways to show four different orders in which the merchandise information might be filed. Pick the answer (A, B, C, or D) in Column II in which the notations are arranged according to the above filing rules.

SAMPLE QUESTION:

COLUMN I

1. Cluney (4865) 6/17/05
2. Roster (2466) 5/10/04
3. Altool (7114) 10/15/05
4. Cluney (5276) 12/18/04
5. Cluney (4865) 4/8/05

COLUMN II

A. 2, 3, 4, 1, 5
B. 2, 5, 1, 3, 4
C. 3, 2, 1, 4, 5
D. 3, 5, 1, 4, 2

The CORRECT way to file the cards is:

   3. *Altool (7114) 10/15/05*
   5. *Cluney (4865) 4/8/05*
   1. *Cluney (4865) 6/17/05*
   4. *Cluney (5276) 12/18/04*
   2. *Roster (2466) 5/10/04*

Since the correct filing order is 3, 5, 1, 4, 2, the answer to the sample question is D.

	COLUMN I		COLUMN II	
9.	1. Warren (96063) 3/30/06 2. Moore (21237) 9/4/07 3. Newman (10050) 12/12/06 4. Downs (81251) 1/2/06 5. Oliver (60145) 6/30/07		A. 2, 4, 3, 5, 1 B. 2, 3, 5, 4, 1 C. 4, 5, 2, 3, 1 D. 4, 2, 3, 5, 1	9.____
10.	1. Henry (40552) 7/6/07 2. Boyd (91251) 9/1/06 3. George (8196) 12/12/06 4. George (31096) 1/12/07 5. West (6109) 8/9/06		A. 5, 4, 3, 1, 2 B. 2, 3, 4, 1, 5 C. 2, 4, 3, 1, 5 D. 5, 2, 3, 1, 4	10.____
11.	1. Salba (4670) 9/7/06 2. Salba (51219) 3/1/06 3. Crete (81562) 7/1/07 4. Salba (51219) 1/11/07 5. Texi (31549) 1/25/06		A. 5, 3, 1, 2, 4 B. 3, 1, 2, 4, 5 C. 3, 5, 4, 2, 1 D. 5, 3, 4, 2, 1	11.____
12.	1. Crayone (87105) 6/10/07 2. Shamba (49210) 1/5/06 3. Valiant (3152) 5/1/07 4. Valiant (3152) 1/9/07 5. Poro (59613) 7/1/06		A. 1, 2, 5, 3, 4 B. 1, 5, 2, 3, 4 C. 1, 5, 3, 4, 2 D. 1, 5, 2, 4, 3	12.____
13.	1. Mackie (42169) 12/20/06 2. Lebo (5198) 9/12/05 3. Drummon (99631) 9/9/07 4. Lebo (15311) 1/25/05 5. Harvin (81765) 6/2/06		A. 3, 2, 1, 5, 4 B. 3, 2, 4, 5, 1 C. 3, 5, 2, 4, 1 D. 3, 5, 4, 2, 1	13.____

Questions 14-18.

DIRECTIONS: Questions 14 through 18 are to be answered on the basis of the following information.

In order to make sure stock is properly located, incoming units are stored as follows:

Stock Numbers	Bin Numbers
00100 - 39999	D30, L44
40000 - 69999	I4L, D38
70000 - 99999	41L, 80D
100000 and over	614, 83D

Using the above table, choose the answer (A, B, C, or D) which lists the correct bin number for the stock number given.

14. 17243

    A. 41L B. 83D C. I4L D. D30

15. 9219

    A. D38 B. L44 C. 614 D. 41L

16. 90125

    A. 41L B. 614 C. D38 D. D30

17. 10001

    A. L44 B. D38 C. SOD D. 83D

18. 200100

    A. 41L B. I4L C. 83D D. D30

19. A supervisor believes that the current filing systems used in his office are not efficient. When his superior goes on vacation, he intends to change all the filing procedures.
    For a supervisor to undertake this move without his superior's knowledge would GENERALLY be considered

    A. *advisable;* it shows that he has initiative
    B. *inadvisable;* the current filing systems are probably the best
    C. *advisable;* the result will be an increase in productivity
    D. *inadvisable;* the supervisor should be informed of any intended changes

20. Assume that you have been assigned the task of handling all telephone calls at a sanitation garage. After a recent snowstorm, your supervisor informed you that all available personnel have been assigned to snow removal duties. However, you have been receiving numerous telephone calls from the public in regard to unshoveled streets and intersections.
    In handling these calls, it is generally considered good policy by the department to

    A. indicate to the callers that the department is clearing streets off as quickly as possible
    B. tell the callers there is nothing that can be done
    C. tell the callers that they are tying up departmental telephones with needless complaints
    D. promise the callers that streets will be cleared by the evening

KEY (CORRECT ANSWERS)

1. B
2. C
3. B
4. D
5. C

6. A
7. C
8. C
9. D
10. B

11. B
12. D
13. C
14. D
15. B

16. A
17. A
18. C
19. D
20. A

TEST 2

DIRECTIONS: Each question or incomplete statement is followed by several suggested answers or completions. Select the one that BEST answers the question or completes the statement. *PRINT THE LETTER OF TEE CORRECT ANSWER IN THE SPACE AT THE RIGHT.*

Questions 1-10.

DIRECTIONS: Questions 1 through 10 are to be answered on the basis of the following information.

A code number for any item is obtained by combining the date of delivery, number of units received, and number of units used.

The first two digits represent the day of the month, the third and fourth digits represent the month, and the fifth and sixth digits represent the year.

The number following the letter R represents the number of units received and the number following the letter U represents the number of units used.

For example, the code number 120673-R5690-U1001 indicates that a delivery of 5,690 units was made on June 12, of which 1,001 units were used.

Using the chart below, answer Questions 1 through 6 by choosing the letter (A, B, C, or D) in which the supplier and stock number correspond to the code number given.

Supplier	Stock Number	Number of Units Received	Delivery Date	Number of Units Used
Stony	38390	8300	May 11	3800
Stoney	39803	1780	September 15	1703
Nievo	21220	5527	October 10	5007
Nieve	38903	1733	August 5	1703
Monte	39213	5527	October 10	5007
Stony	38890	3308	December 9	3300
Stony	83930	3880	September 12	380
Nevo	47101	485	June 11	231
Nievo	12122	5725	May 11	5201
Neve	47101	9721	August 15	8207
Nievo	21120	2275	January 7	2175
Rosa	41210	3821	March 3	2710
Stony	38890	3308	September 12	3300
Dinal	54921	1711	April 2	1117
Stony	33890	8038	March 5	3300
Dinal	54721	1171	March 2	717
Claridge	81927	3308	April 5	3088
Nievo	21122	4878	June 7	3492
Haley	39670	8300	December 23	5300

1. Code No. 120972-R3308-U3300   1.____

    A. Nievo - 12122   B. Stony - 83930
    C. Nievo - 21220   D. Stony - 38890

2. Code No. 101072-R5527-U5007

   A. Nievo - 21220 B. Haley - 39670
   C. Monte - 39213 D. Claridge - 81927

3. Code No. 101073-R5527-U5007

   A. Nievo - 21220 B. Monte - 39213
   C. Nievo - 12122 D. Nievo - 21120

4. Code No. 110573-R5725-U5201

   A. Nievo - 12122 B. Nievo - 21220
   C. Haley - 39670 D. Stony - 38390

5. Code No. 070172-R2275-U2175

   A. Stony - 33890 B. Stony - 83930
   C. Stony - 38390 D. Nievo - 21120

6. Code No. 120972-R3880-U380

   A. Stony - 83930 B. Stony - 38890
   C. Stony - 33890 D. Monte - 39213

Using the same chart, answer Questions 7 through 10, choosing the letter (A, B, C, or D) in which the code number corresponds to the supplier and stock number given.

7. Nieve - 38903

   A. 951973-R1733-U1703 B. 080572-R1733-U1703
   C. 080573-R1733-U1703 D. 050873-R1733-U1703

8. Nevo - 47101

   A. 081573-R9721-U8207 B. 091573-R9721-U8207]
   C. 110672-R485-U231   D. 061172-R485-U231

9. Dinal - 54921

   A. 020473-R1711-U1117 B. 030272-R1171-U717
   C. 020372-R1171-U717   D. 421973-R1711-U1117

10. Nievo - 21122

    A. 070672-R4878-U3492 B. 060772-R4878-U349
    C. 761972-R4878-U3492 D. 060772-R4878-U3492

11. A citizen who has called the office at which you are working has started yelling on the telephone. He is annoyed because he has been switched from office to office and still has not reached the proper party.
    Of the following, the BEST practice to follow is to

    A. hang up on this individual since he is obviously a troublemaker
    B. yell back at him for being so childish
    C. tell him that you have heard that complaint before
    D. try to calm this person and help him reach the proper party

12. Which of the following is the MOST likely result of employees publicly criticizing the activities of their agency?
The

    A. employees will be terminated for the good of the agency
    B. public's respect for the agency may decrease
    C. productive members of the agency may resign
    D. agency may sue these employees for libel

13. It is essential for city employees who deal with the public to provide service as promptly and completely as possible.
Letters from the public lodging complaints regarding poor service should GENERALLY be handled by

    A. answering them as soon as possible according to agency procedures
    B. ignoring them, since only troublemakers usually write such letters
    C. returning them, since the city government does not respond to public complaints
    D. acknowledging them with no further action necessary

14. While checking the work of a clerk who is under your supervision, you notice that he has made the same mistake a number of times.
In order to help prevent this clerk from making the same mistake again, it would be BEST for you to take which of the following courses of action?

    A. Correct the errors yourself and not mention it to the clerk
    B. Provide training for the clerk
    C. Reprimand the clerk for the mistakes made
    D. Remind the clerk of the errors he has previously made

15. A community resident calls the sanitation garage in which you are working to inquire about the days in which old furniture can be put on the street for collection. Although your unit is responsible for these collections, you do not have this information and there is nobody in the office to assist you.
Of the following, it would be MOST advisable to

    A. tell the citizen to call back in an hour
    B. get the citizen's telephone number and inform him that you will call back when you get the information
    C. switch the call to another unit and let them get the information
    D. put the caller on hold and try to find someone that has the answer

16. As a supervisor, you have been given the responsibility of maintaining attendance records for your garage. A co-worker, who has been late a number of times, has asked you to overlook his recent lateness since it involves only ten minutes. He has been warned previously for lateness and will receive some kind of disciplinary action because of this recent lateness, for you to overlook the lateness would be

    A. *advisable;* it involves only a matter of ten minutes
    B. *inadvisable;* this employee should have to suffer the consequences of his actions
    C. *advisable;* morale in the unit will improve
    D. *inadvisable;* employee lateness should never be excused

17. When a supervisor answers incoming telephone calls, it is important for him to FIRST

    A. identify himself and/or his office
    B. ask the caller to state the reason for the call
    C. ask the caller the nature of the call
    D. ask the caller to identify himself

18. It appears to you that the current mail distribution procedures are inefficient.
    For you to make a suggestion to your supervisor for the implementation of new procedures, would be

    A. *advisable;* if the supervisor thinks your ideas are worthwhile;they may be implemented
    B. *inadvisable;* supervisors generally are not interested in changing procedures
    C. *advisable;* new procedures generally provide better results than old procedures
    D. *inadvisable;* only methods analysts should suggest changes in procedures

19. As a supervisor, you direct the work of two clerks. Recently, you discovered that one of the two clerks generally loafs around on Friday afternoons. This past Friday, you saw this particular employee standing around conversing with several employees. At that point, you severely reprimanded this employee in the presence of the other employees.
    For you to have reprimanded this employee in such a fashion was

    A. *advisable;* this employee *had it coming*
    B. *inadvisable;* you should have spoken to him privately
    C. *advisable;* this reprimand also served as a warning to the others
    D. *inadvisable;* employees should not be reprimanded

20. As a supervisor, you have been assigned to maintain garage supplies. Recently, a co-worker requested a quantity of nails and screws for use in his home. Since this involves only a small amount of supplies, he felt it would not be wrong to make such a request.
    In this case, it would be ADVISABLE for you to

    A. give the co-worker the supplies
    B. remind the co-worker that city supplies are only for city use
    C. notify the investigation department in regard to this employee
    D. forget the incident

KEY (CORRECT ANSWERS)

1.	D	11.	D
2.	C	12.	B
3.	A	13.	A
4.	A	14.	B
5.	D	15.	B
6.	A	16.	B
7.	D	17.	A
8.	C	18.	A
9.	A	19.	B
10.	A	20.	B

EXAMINATION SECTION
TEST 1

DIRECTIONS: Each question or incomplete statement is followed by several suggested answers or completions. Select the one that BEST answers the question or completes the statement. *PRINT THE LETTER OF THE CORRECT ANSWER IN THE SPACE AT THE RIGHT.*

1. The process of determining the quantity of goods and materials that are in stock is commonly called

    A. receiving
    B. disbursement
    C. reconciliation
    D. inventory

2. Proper and effective storage procedure involves the storing of

    A. items together on the basis of class grouping
    B. all items in chronological order based on date received
    C. items in alphabetical order based on date of delivery
    D. items randomly wherever space is available

3. Which of the following is the FIRST step involved in correctly taking an inventory?

    A. Reconciliation of inventory records with the number of items on hand
    B. Analysis of possible discrepancies between items on hand and the stock record balance
    C. Identification and recording of the locations of all items in stock
    D. Issuance of an inventory directive to all vendors

4. Supply items other than food which are subject to deterioration should be checked

    A. at delivery time only
    B. occasionally
    C. only when issued
    D. periodically

5. For which of the following supplies is it MOST necessary to provide ample ventilation?

    A. Small rubber parts
    B. Metal products
    C. Flammable liquids
    D. Wooden items

6. Storing small lots of supplies in an area designated for the storage of large lots of supplies will generally result in

    A. *loss* of supplies
    B. *loss* of storage space
    C. *increase* in inventory
    D. *increase* in storage space

7. Compliance with fire preventive measures is a major requirement for the maintenance of a safe warehouse. Which of the following statements is LEAST important in describing a measure useful in maintaining a fire preventive facility?

    A. Smoking is only permitted in designated areas.
    B. Oil-soaked rags should be disposed of promptly and not stored.
    C. When not in use, electrical machinery should be grounded.
    D. Gasoline-powered materials handling equipment should not be refueled with the motor running.

8. It is POOR storage practice to store small valuable items loosely in open containers in bulk storage areas because doing so results in the

   A. misplacement of such items
   B. pilferage of these items
   C. deterioration of such supplies
   D. hindrance in inspection of these supplies

9. Assume that you have been placed in charge of the receiving operations at your garage. Generally, you receive all the supplies you order during the first week of each month. Of the following, the MOST effective and economic way to facilitate receiving operations would be to

   A. secure overtime authorization for laborers during that week
   B. have all truck deliveries made in one day
   C. stagger truck deliveries throughout each morning of the week
   D. assign all personnel to receiving duty for that week

10. Effective security measures must be instituted to provide for the safekeeping of city supplies.
    However, the scope and complexity of security measures used at a warehouse facility should correspond MOST NEARLY to the

    A. value of supplies stored in the warehouse
    B. borough in which the warehouse is located
    C. level of warehouse activity
    D. age of the warehouse facility

11. To facilitate handling and issuance of supply items that have a high turnover rate, they should generally be stored

    A. away from accessible aisles
    B. on upper shelves
    C. in a locked compartment area
    D. close to the service counter area

12. The MOST important factor to be considered in effectively storing heavy, bulky, and difficult-to-handle items is to store these items

    A. as close to shipping areas as possible
    B. in storage areas with a low floor-load capacity
    C. only in outside storage sheds
    D. away from aisles

Questions 13-16.

DIRECTIONS: Questions 13 through 16 are to be answered using ONLY the information in the following passage.

Fire exit drills should be established and held periodically to effectively train personnel to leave their working area promptly upon proper signal and to evacuate the building speedily but without confusion. All fire exit drills should be carefully planned and carried out in a serious manner under rigid discipline so as to provide positive protection in the event of a real emergency. As a general rule, the local fire department should be furnished advance information regarding the exact date and time the exit drill is scheduled. When it is impossible to hold regular drills, written instructions should be distributed to all employees.

Depending upon individual circumstances, fires in warehouses vary from those of fast development that are almost instantly beyond any possibility of employee control to others of relatively slow development where a small readily attackable flame may be present for periods of time up to 15 minutes or more during which simple attack with fire extinguishers or small building hoses may prevent the fire development. In any case, it is characteristic of many warehouse fires that at a certain point in development they flash up to the top of the stack, increase heat quickly, and spread rapidly. There is a degree of inherent danger in attacking warehouse type fires and all employees should be thoroughly trained in the use of the types of extinguishers or small hoses in the buildings and well instructed in the necessity of always staying between the fire and a direct pass to an exit.

13. Employees should be instructed that, when fighting a fire, they MUST

    A. try to control the blaze
    B. extinguish any fire in 15 minutes
    C. remain between the fire and a direct passage to the exit
    D. keep the fire between themselves and the fire exit

14. Whenever conditions are such that regular fire drills cannot be held, then which one of the following actions should be taken?

    A. The local fire department should be notified.
    B. Rigid discipline should be maintained during work hours.
    C. Personnel should be instructed to leave their working area by whatever means are available.
    D. Employees should receive fire drill procedures in writing.

15. The passage indicates that the purpose of fire exit drills is to train employees to

    A. control a fire before it becomes uncontrollable
    B. act as firefighters
    C. leave the working area promptly
    D. be serious

16. According to the passage, fire exit drills will prove to be of *utmost* effectiveness if

    A. employee participation is made voluntary
    B. they take place periodically
    C. the fire department actively participates
    D. they are held without advance planning

Questions 17-20.

DIRECTIONS: Questions 17 through 20 are to be answered using ONLY the information in the following paragraph.

A report is frequently ineffective because the person writing it is not fully acquainted with all the necessary details before he actually starts to construct the report. All details pertaining to the subject should be known before the report is started. If the essential facts are not known, they should be investigated. It is wise to have essential facts written down rather than to depend too much on memory, especially if the facts pertain to such matters as amounts, dates, names of persons, or other specific data. When the necessary information has been gathered, the general plan and content of the report should be thought out before the writing is actually begun. A person with little or no experience in writing reports may find that it is wise to make a brief outline. Persons with more experience should not need a written outline, but they should make mental notes of the steps they are to follow. If writing reports without dictation is a regular part of an office worker's duties, he should set aside a certain time during the day when he is least likely to be interrupted. That may be difficult, but in most offices there are certain times in the day when the callers, telephone calls, and other interruptions are not numerous. During those times, it is best to write reports that need undivided concentration. Reports that are written amid a series of interruptions may be poorly done.

17. Before starting to write an effective report, it is necessary to

    A. memorize all specific information
    B. disregard ambiguous data
    C. know all pertinent information
    D. develop a general plan

18. Reports dealing with complex and difficult material should be

    A. prepared and written by the supervisor of the unit
    B. written when there is the least chance of interruption
    C. prepared and written as part of regular office routine
    D. outlined and then dictated

19. According to the passage, employees with no prior familiarity in writing reports may find it helpful to

    A. prepare a brief outline
    B. mentally prepare a synopsis of the report's content
    C. have a fellow employee help in writing the report
    D. consult previous reports

20. In writing a report, needed information which is unclear should be

    A. disregarded   B. investigated
    C. memorized   D. gathered

KEY (CORRECT ANSWERS)

1.	D	11.	D
2.	A	12.	A
3.	C	13.	C
4.	D	14.	D
5.	C	15.	C
6.	B	16.	B
7.	C	17.	C
8.	B	18.	B
9.	C	19.	A
10.	A	20.	B

TEST 2

DIRECTIONS: Each question or incomplete statement is followed by several suggested answers or completions. Select the one that BEST answers the question or completes the statement. *PRINT THE LETTER OF THE CORRECT ANSWER IN THE SPACE AT THE RIGHT.*

Questions 1-4.

DIRECTIONS: Questions 1 through 4 are to be answered using ONLY the information in the following passage.

The operation and maintenance of the stock-location system is a warehousing function and responsibility. The stock locator system shall consist of a file of stock-location record cards, either manually or mechanically prepared, depending upon the equipment available. The file shall contain an individual card for each stock item stored in the depot, with the records maintained in stock number sequence.

The locator file is used for all receiving, warehousing, inventory, and shipping activities in the depot. The locator file must contain complete and accurate data to provide ready support to the various depot functions and activities, i.e., processing shipping documents, updating records on mechanized equipment, where applicable, supplying accurate locator information for stock selection and proper storage of receipts, consolidating storage locations of identical items not subject to shelf-life control, and preventing the consolidation of stock of limited shelf-life items. The file is also essential in accomplishing location surveys and the inventory program.

Storage of bulk stock items by "spot-location" method is generally recognized as the best means of obtaining maximum warehouse space utilization. Despite the fact that the spot-location method of storage enables full utilization of storage capacity, this method may prove inefficient unless it is supplemented by adequate stock-location control, including proper lay-out and accurate maintenance of stock locator cards.

1. The manner in which the stock-location record cards should be filed is

    A. alphabetically   B. chronologically
    C. numerically   D. randomly

1.____

2. Items of limited shelf-life should

    A. not be stored
    B. not be stored together
    C. be stored in stock sequence
    D. be stored together

2.____

3. Which one of the following is NOT mentioned in the passage as a use of the stock-location system?
   Aids in

    A. accomplishing location surveys
    B. providing information for stock selection
    C. storing items received for the first time
    D. processing shipping documents

3.____

4. If the spot-location method of storing is used, then the use of the stock-location system is

   A. *desirable,* because the stock-location system is recognized as the best means of obtaining maximum warehouse space utilization
   B. *undesirable,* because additional records must be kept
   C. *desirable,* because stock-location controls are necessary with the spot-location storage method
   D. *undesirable,* because a stock-locator system will take up valuable storage space

Questions 5-8.

DIRECTIONS: Questions 5 through 8 are to be answered using ONLY the information in the following paragraph.

Known damage is defined as damage that is apparent and acknowledged by the carrier at the time of delivery to the purchaser. A meticulous inspection of the damaged goods should be completed by the purchaser and a notation specifying the extent of the damage should be applied to the carrier's original freight bill. As is the case in known loss, it is necessary for the carrier's agent to acknowledge by signature the damage notation in order for it to have any legal status. The purchaser should not refuse damaged freight since it is his legal duty to accept the property and to employ every available and reasonable means to protect the shipment and minimize the loss. Acceptance of a damaged shipment does not endanger any legitimate claim the purchaser may have against the carrier for damage. If the purchaser fails to observe the legal duty to accept damaged freight, the carrier may consider it abandoned. After properly notifying the vendor and purchaser of his intentions, the carrier may dispose of the material at public sale.

5. Before disposing of an abandoned shipment, the carrier must

   A. notify the vendor and the carrier's agent
   B. advise the vendor and purchaser of his plans
   C. notify the purchaser and the carrier's agent
   D. obtain the signature of the carrier's agent on the freight bill

6. In the case of damaged freight, the original freight bill will only have legal value if it is signed by the

   A. carrier's agent   B. purchaser
   C. vendor   D. purchaser and vendor

7. A purchaser does not protect a shipment of cargo that is damaged and is further deteriorating.
   According to the above paragraph, the action of the purchaser is

   A. *acceptable,* because he is not obligated to protect damaged cargo
   B. *unacceptable,* because damaged cargo must be protected no matter what is involved
   C. *acceptable,* because he took possession of the cargo
   D. *unacceptable,* because he is obligated by law to protect the cargo

8. The TWO requirements that must be satisfied before cargo can be labeled *known damage* are signs of evident damage and

   A. confirmation by the carrier or carrier's agent that this is so
   B. delayed shipment of goods
   C. signature of acceptance by the purchaser
   D. acknowledgment by the vendor that this is so

Questions 9-13.

DIRECTIONS: Questions 9 through 13 are to be answered on the basis of the following graph.

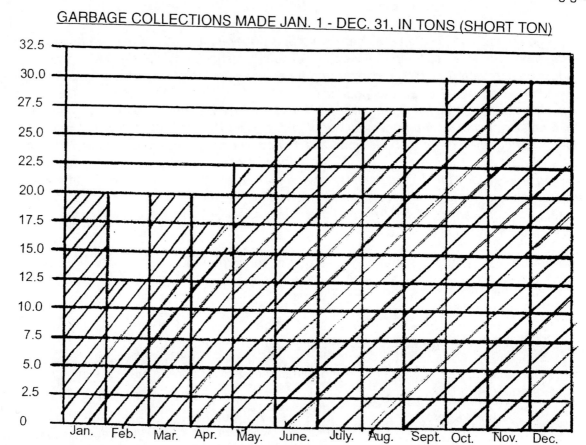

9. According to the information presented in the graph, the weight of the average monthly collection of garbage is MOST NEARLY _____ tons.

   A. 22.5
   B. 23.5
   C. 24.5
   D. 25.5

10. If a truck can carry 6,000 lbs., then the number of truck-loads collected during the year was MOST NEARLY

    A. 55
    B. 75
    C. 95
    D. 115

11. The amount of garbage collected during the second half of the year represents APPROXIMATELY what percentage of the total garbage collected during the year?

    A. 50%
    B. 60%
    C. 70%
    D. 80%

12. During the months of September, October, and November, approximately 12% of the collections consisted of fallen leaves.
What was the weight of the remaining garbage NOT containing fallen leaves for that period?
_____ tons.

   A. 10   B. 20   C. 65   D. 75

13. Assume that the collections for the year as shown in the above graph exceeded the previous year's collection by 17%. The collection made in the previous year was MOST NEARLY _____ tons.

   A. 50   B. 225   C. 240   D. 275

Questions 14-17.

DIRECTIONS: Questions 14 through 17 are to be answered on the basis of the following graph

INVENTORY LEVELS (IN DOZENS) OF ITEM A IN STOREHOUSE AT BEGINNING OF MONTH FOR A PERIOD OF TWELVS MONTH

14. The average monthly inventory level during the course of the year was MOST NEARLY _____ dozen.

   A. 45   B. 60   C. 75   D. 90

15. If one dozen items fit in a carton measuring 2 feet by 2 feet by 3 feet, what MINIMUM volume would be required to store the maximum August inventory?
_____ cubic feet.

   A. 12   B. 100   C. 700   D. 1,200

16. Assume that deliveries are made to the storehouse on the first working day of each month. If 30% of the June inventory was consumed during the month, how many items had to be delivered to reach the July inventory level?
    _____ items.

    A. 288 B. 408 C. 696 D. 1,080

17. Which three-month period contained the LOWEST average inventory level?

    A. Jan., Feb., March
    B. April, May, June
    C. July, Aug., Sept.
    D. Oct., Nov., Dec.

18. Assume that it takes approximately 1 1/2 minutes to unload a dozen identical items from a delivery truck.
    At this speed, the amount of time it should take to unload a shipment of 876 items is MOST NEARLY _____ minutes.

    A. 90 B. 100 C. 110 D. 120

19. Assume that a shop clerk has received a bill of $108 for a delivery of clamps which cost $4.32 per dozen.
    How many clamps should there be in this delivery?

    A. 25 B. 36 C. 300 D. 360

20. Employee A has not used any leave time and has accumulated a total of 45 leave days. How many months did it take Employee A to have accumulated 45 leave days if the accrual rate is 1 2/3 days per month?

    A. 25 B. 27 C. 29 D. 31

KEY (CORRECT ANSWERS)

1. C		11. B	
2. B		12. D	
3. C		13. C	
4. C		14. B	
5. B		15. D	
6. A		16. B	
7. D		17. D	
8. A		18. C	
9. B		19. C	
10. C		20. B	

EXAMINATION SECTION
TEST 1

DIRECTIONS: Each question or incomplete statement is followed by several suggested answers or completions. Select the one that BEST answers the question or completes the statement. *PRINT THE LETTER OF THE CORRECT ANSWER IN THE SPACE AT THE RIGHT.*

1. The MOST important reason for rotating stock is that

   A. issuance of the newest stock first guarantees that using agencies will generally receive stock in good condition
   B. this practice allocates delivery of stock to each agency on an equal basis
   C. older stock is issued first, thereby reducing spoilage in storage areas
   D. older stock is sold as scrap

    1.____

2. A piece of equipment that is used to stack items at various heights above ground level is a

   A. forklift truck   B. gravity roller conveyor
   C. hydraulic handtruck   D. skid

    2.____

3. Frozen foods are likely to deteriorate unless proper storage conditions are maintained. Which one of the following is generally the LEAST important factor to be taken into consideration when storing these foods?

   A. Temperature   B. Light
   C. Humidity   D. Air circulation

    3.____

4. Vapors given off by flammable liquids in storage are dangerous because the vapors burn easily.
   To reduce the danger presented by stored flammable liquids, it is MOST advisable to

   A. store these liquids in warm areas such as the boiler room
   B. install curbs which can direct spilled flammable liquids away from the storage area and into other sections of the stockroom
   C. locate the storage area for these liquids in the center of the stockroom away from doors and windows to limit air circulation
   D. inspect the containers of flammable liquids for leaks at regular intervals during the year

    4.____

5. Receiving, storage, and shipping operations are more effectively carried out if items are handled in unit loads. A unit load consists of two or more small items handled as a single unit.
   The MOST important advantage of using unit loads in store-room operations is that

   A. mechanized materials handling equipment can be used more effectively
   B. manual handling of individual items is necessary
   C. use of pallets is not required
   D. more effective use of stock items is made by using agencies

    5.____

6. In order to reduce spoilage of food items caused by insects and vermin, it would be MOST advisable to

   A. make a thorough inspection every year or so in order to see if there is infestation
   B. inspect the food weekly and take swift action to get rid of any insects or vermin present

    6.____

C. only check incoming food items for signs of infestation
D. keep windows and doors tightly shut so that insects and vermin do not enter the stockroom

7. Oils should generally be used in areas that are

   A. cool and well-ventilated
   B. warm and well-ventilated
   C. cool but not ventilated
   D. warm but not ventilated

8. The LEAST important factor to be considered when choosing a piece of equipment for moving stock in the stockroom is generally the stock item's

   A. size   B. shape   C. value   D. weight

9. In most instances, when a stockman refers to the term *floor load capacity* of a storage area, he means the

   A. height to which stock can be stacked
   B. weight that can be stored
   C. area that can be used for storage purposes
   D. quantity of stock that may be stored

10. The one of the following statements which is CORRECT in regard to storing stock on pallets is that this practice

    A. has been shown to increase physical damage to stock
    B. does not permit stacking of stock
    C. allows stock to be moved more quickly and easily than stock that is not stored on pallets

11. A stockman has been given responsibility for supervising the following operations:
    I. Transporting fresh fruit from the loading dock to the storage area
    II. Transporting fresh vegetables from the loading dock to an outdoor conveyor belt
    III. Transporting frozen vegetables from the loading dock to an indoor refrigerated area
    IV. Storing metal pipes in an outdoor storage area
    Gasoline-powered forklift trucks should be used for Operation(s)

    A. I and II, but not III and IV
    B. III and IV, but not I and II
    C. III, but not I, II, and IV
    D. IV, but not I, II, and III

12. Transporting commodities with the use of a conveyor belt is generally MOST appropriate for items packed in

    A. small packages with flat surfaces
    B. 55-gallon drums
    C. heavy, bulky, and irregularly sized packages
    D. metal cylinders

13. Assume that six 20-pound packages are to be moved to a storage area one-hundred feet away.
Which one of the following indicates the MOST efficient use of stockroom employees and equipment?

   A. Two assistant stockmen each carry one package at a time from the loading dock to the storage area
   B. An assistant stockman carries one box at a time from the loading dock to the storage area
   C. An assistant stockman transports all the packages from the loading dock to the storage area with the aid of an electric handtruck in one trip
   D. An assistant stockman transports all the packages from the loading dock to the storage area with the aid of a forklift truck in one trip

14. The factor which is of LEAST importance in determining the maximum height to which stock can be stored is the

   A. type of materials handling equipment that is available
   B. type of stock being stored
   C. strength of the containers in which the stock items are packed
   D. floor load capacity of the storage area

15. The quantity and type of stock delivered to the stockroom must be verified and reconciled with the stockroom purchase order or requisition order.
This function should be performed when the stock is

   A. distributed   B. inventoried
   C. received   D. stored

16. Circulating air may be damaging to some stock kept in long-term storage.
Under normal conditions, which one of the following would NOT be damaged by circulating air?

   A. Tires   B. Cement
   C. Inner tubes   D. Dried fruits

17. If the brake system on a forklift truck is not in working order, you should

   A. *drive* the forklift truck out of the storage area
   B. *drive* the forklift truck very slowly while transporting stock
   C. *not drive* the forklift truck until the brakes are in working order
   D. *drive* the forklift truck in reverse while moving the stock

18. To reduce deterioration of fiber rope kept in storage, it is necessary to keep the storage area

   A. cool, dry, and well-ventilated
   B. warm, dry, and well-ventilated
   C. warm, damp, and well-ventilated
   D. cool and damp, but not ventilated

19. The use of an adjustable receiving dock is

    A. *undesirable*, because the adjustments that must be made are too complicated for most employees
    B. *undesirable*, because the differences in the heights of most truck body floors are very small, so there is no need for an adjustable receiving dock
    C. *desirable*, because it can be adjusted to match the height of most truck body floors, so that receiving operations are simplified
    D. *desirable*, because it eliminates the need for most other materials handling equipment

20. The net balance of paper is greater this week than it was last week.
    This is an indication that the quantity of paper

    A. issued was *greater* than the quantity received
    B. received was *greater* than the quantity issued
    C. issued was the *same* as the quantity received
    D. remained the *same* after all other stock transactions

21. Items with high turnover rates should generally be stored

    A. in outdoor storage areas
    B. close to shipping or dispensing areas
    C. at the vendor's premises and delivered to using agencies
    D. on pallets located in motor vehicles

22. The requisitioning of too much of any item is considered poor stockkeeping practice.
    The LEAST harmful result of such a practice is the

    A. deterioration or spoilage of some items
    B. excessive allocation of storage space to one commodity
    C. excessive record keeping
    D. possible loss of items because they may become obsolete

23. An inspector from the comptroller's office has the responsibility of determining whether the quality of delivered stock is acceptable.
    In order to insure that a representative sample of a shipment of delivered stock is available for inspection, that stock should NOT be

    A. issued   B. protected   C. counted   D. stacked

24. When you are receiving stock, it is LEAST important to check for

    A. quantity   B. quality
    C. nomenclature   D. monetary value

25. Some stock is issued in less-than-unit pack quantities.
    The advantage of having a *loose-issue bin* section is that

    A. there is less chance of pilferage from bin sections
    B. using agencies do not have to order more stock than they need
    C. storing of a large quantity of loose stock is easier than bulk storage
    D. checking of such stock is not necessary

26. Assuming that space is available, the storage of empty wooden pallets in storerooms should   26._____
    A. be the minimum number required for storeroom operations
    B. be the maximum number that can be stored
    C. be allowed only in emergencies
    D. depend on the size of the pallets

27. When driving a forklift truck, greater load stability is obtained by keeping the forks as _____ as possible and carrying the load as _____ as possible.   27._____
    A. wide apart; high
    B. wide apart; close to the ground
    C. close together; high
    D. close together; close to the ground

28. In order to keep spare batteries for electrically-powered materials handling equipment in a usable condition, the batteries should   28._____
    A. be charged every two or three months
    B. be charged every other week after adding acid to them
    C. be tested every six months
    D. have their battery cells replaced every three or four months

29. Office machines held in storage are LEAST affected by   29._____
    A. rust   B. corrosion
    C. infestation   D. dust

30. Metals and metal products should NOT be stored in areas of   30._____
    A. high temperature   B. low temperature
    C. high humidity   D. low humidity

KEY (CORRECT ANSWERS)

1.	C	16.	D
2.	A	17.	C
3.	B	18.	A
4.	D	19.	C
5.	A	20.	B
6.	B	21.	B
7.	A	22.	C
8.	C	23.	A
9.	B	24.	D
10.	C	25.	B
11.	D	26.	A
12.	A	27.	B
13.	C	28.	A
14.	B	29.	C
15.	C	30.	C

TEST 2

DIRECTIONS: Each question or incomplete statement is followed by several suggested answers or completions. Select the one that BEST answers the question or completes the statement. *PRINT THE LETTER OF THE CORRECT ANSWER IN THE SPACE AT THE RIGHT.*

1. Which one of the following generally has the SHORTEST shelf life, if storage conditions are the same for all items and the temperature is kept at 70° F?

    A. Canned tomato juice
    B. Canned corn
    C. Cornstarch
    D. Noodles

    1.____

2. If the following four stock shipments, delivered the first week of June, are to be moved from the receiving dock to the storage area, the one that should be moved FIRST is

    A. frozen fish
    B. color television units
    C. automobile parts
    D. electric drills

    2.____

3. Taking an inventory should enable you to determine the exact number of items in storage.
    However, the inventory CANNOT help you determine whether

    A. the latest stock record balances are accurate
    B. adjustments should be made in stock records
    C. maximum or minimum levels of stock have been reached
    D. the stock is being used properly

    3.____

4. It is advisable to keep storerooms clean of debris that might accumulate from storeroom operations.
    Generally, the BEST time in which to perform such cleanup operations is

    A. at the end of each working day
    B. before any major storekeeping activity is to be performed
    C. at the end of any storekeeping activity in which debris is accumulated
    D. at the time that a periodic inventory is taken

    4.____

5. Which type of fire extinguisher should be used on a fire that develops in operating electrical equipment?
    _____ extinguisher.

    A. Soda acid
    B. Foam
    C. Carbon dioxide
    D. Antifreeze type

    5.____

6. A vendor delivers eleven cartons of linseed oil, each carton containing 12 quarts. The original order called for a delivery of thirty gallons of this oil.
    The quantity of oil delivered was _____ gallons _____ than the quantity ordered.

    A. three; more
    B. twelve; more
    C. three; less
    D. twelve; less

    6.____

7. A spot check of the perpetual inventory indicates that there are four packs of No. 2 pencils and seven packs of No. 3 pencils in stock, each pack containing six dozen pencils.
    The TOTAL number of pencils is _____ pencils.

    A. 168
    B. 336
    C. 792
    D. 876

    7.____

8. On Monday, four employees each worked three hours overtime; on Tuesday, three employees each worked two hours overtime; on Wednesday, four employees each worked two and one-half hours overtime.
   The TOTAL number of overtime hours worked by ALL employees is _____ hours.

   A. 22   B. 27 1/2   C. 28   D. 33

9. From a 500-foot coil of wire, the following pieces were cut off and used for repair work: 37 feet 6 inches, 35 feet, 73 feet 6 inches, 83 feet 6 inches, and 47 feet.
   The length of wire LEFT is _____ feet _____ inches.

   A. 223; 6   B. 276; 6   C. 304; 0   D. 385; 6

10. A delivery truck containing 672 packages has arrived at the receiving dock.
    How many assistant stockmen are needed to unload this truck in two hours, if one assistant stockman can unload 42 packages an hour?

    A. 8   B. 10   C. 12   D. 16

11. The following quantities of turpentine were taken out of a full 55-gallon drum: 7 pints; 9 pints; 17 pints; 23 pints; 48 pints.
    The amount of turpentine REMAINING in the 55-gallon drum is _____ gallons.

    A. 13   B. 26   C. 42   D. 46

12. Ten cartons, each containing twenty-five 1-pound packages of steel wool, are delivered to your stockroom.
    If steel wool costs $0.567 per pound, the TOTAL cost of this steel wool in this delivery is

    A. $5.67   B. $14.18   C. $131.75   D. $141.75

13. A shipment of three hundred fifty 40-pound bags of charcoal briquettes has been unloaded onto the receiving platform. The bags must be moved to the storage area on a handtruck which has a carrying capacity of 560 pounds. How many trips will it take to move all the bags if the handtruck is loaded to capacity on each trip?

    A. 20   B. 25   C. 30   D. 35

14. The storekeeper tells you to order 15% less automobile anti-freeze this year than the 23,000 gallons of this item that was ordered last year.
    The amount of automobile anti-freeze you should order is MOST NEARLY _____ gallons.

    A. 13,500   B. 15,500   C. 18,000   D. 19,500

15. There are five 25-pound packages of salt in a container.
    What is the GREATEST number of containers that can be kept in a storage area that can hold 296,250 pounds?

    A. 125   B. 2,370   C. 11,850   D. 59,250

16. A 10% discount is given on orders that are paid within 15 days of delivery.
    What is the amount of the discount on an order of 25 mops, if the cost per mop is $7.74?

    A. $2.50   B. $19.35   C. $25.00   D. $77.40

17. A 3-foot length of pipe covering is priced at $1.53.
If you have ordered 447 feet of pipe covering, the TOTAL price for this order is MOST NEARLY

    A. $76   B. $228   C. $684   D. $730

18. You notice that of the 73 cartons that were just unloaded, 23 are seriously damaged but the remaining cartons are acceptable.
If each carton contains 16 packages weighing 8 ounces each, then the TOTAL net weight of the acceptable items is _____ pounds.

    A. 184   B. 368   C. 400   D. 584

19. If the first one hundred pounds of an item costs $0.78 per pound and each additional pound costs $0.75, what is the cost of 215 pounds of this item?

    A. $161.25   B. $164.25   C. $166.50   D. $167.70

20. Suppose your records indicate that the following quantities of a commodity were ordered: 8 dozen items in January; 7 dozen items in February; 7 dozen items in March; 2 dozen items in April; 1 dozen items in May; and 1 dozen items in June.
The AVERAGE monthly order for these months is approximately _____ per month.

    A. 26   B. 52   C. 104   D. 312

21. Suppose that thirty-four cartons containing twenty-four 1-quart cans and seventy-eight cartons containing eight 1-gallon cans of a commodity have been ordered.
If the price of one quart is $.10, what is the approximate TOTAL cost of this order?

    A. $62   B. $82   C. $250   D. $331

22. Listed below are four orders you have received. Which of these orders CANNOT be filled completely from a 250-foot coil of wire? _____ pieces, each one _____ feet _____ inches in length.

    A. 27; 8; 4   B. 30; 8; 3   C. 33; 7; 8   D. 34; 7; 3

23. Suppose that Portland cement is issued in bags weighing 94 pounds each.
If a repair job requires the use of 2,310 pounds of cement, then the MINIMUM number of bags that should be ordered is

    A. 23   B. 24   C. 25   D. 26

24. A spot check of the perpetual inventory indicates that there are 288 pads of writing paper.
How many weeks would you be able to fill orders if 35 pads are used each week? _____ weeks.

    A. 9   B. 8   C. 7   D. 6

25. An item is packed three to a package, each package weighing 7 pounds. If the shelf on which this item is stored can hold only 133 pounds, what is the MAXIMUM number of packed items that can be stored on the shelf?

    A. 17   B. 20   C. 57   D. 60

KEY (CORRECT ANSWERS)

1. A
2. A
3. D
4. C
5. C

6. A
7. C
8. C
9. A
10. A

11. C
12. D
13. B
14. D
15. B

16. B
17. B
18. C
19. B
20. B

21. D
22. C
23. C
24. B
25. C

EXAMINATION SECTION
TEST 1

DIRECTIONS: Each question or incomplete statement is followed by several suggested answers or completions. Select the one that BEST answers the question or completes the statement. *PRINT THE LETTER OF THE CORRECT ANSWER IN THE SPACE AT THE RIGHT.*

1. The storage life of commodities in common dry storage is dependent in part upon the factors of temperature and humidity.
   In general, the MOST favorable combination of these two factors for storage purposes is _____ temperature and _____ humidity.

   A. high; low
   B. high; high
   C. low; high
   D. low; low

   1.____

2. Which one of the following is it MOST important to locate on the ground floor near the point of receipt?

   A. Difficult-to-handle and bulky items
   B. Items which are readily portable and marketable
   C. Lightweight items
   D. Low turnover items

   2.____

3. A basic reason for assigning commodity code numbers to purchased and stored items is to

   A. prevent pilferage
   B. increase the use of mechanized equipment
   C. facilitate ready reference in communications
   D. decrease flexibility of storage areas

   3.____

4. A straddle carry truck is MOST appropriately used in a warehouse or in a section of a warehouse handling

   A. automotive parts and tools
   B. paints and varnishes
   C. pipe and lumber
   D. stationery and paper

   4.____

5. In general, you would expect to find materials handling equipment to be equipped with solid rubber tires when used primarily

   A. for heavy-duty lifting, both indoors and outdoors
   B. for indoor operations
   C. in improved outdoor storage areas
   D. in unimproved outdoor storage areas

   5.____

6. Of the following, the MOST probable hazard in storing subsistence supplies, such as meats and cereal products, is

   A. breakage
   B. flammability
   C. spillage
   D. spoilage

   6.____

7. When operating a forklift truck, the one of the following which is LEAST hazardous is

   A. backing the truck slowly down a slight grade or ramp
   B. driving the truck with the forks highly elevated
   C. leaving the truck unattended, facing downhill, with the motor running
   D. trying to lift large loads with only one fork

8. Of the following, the one which is usually LEAST likely to be shown on properly maintained bin tags is the

   A. amount received   B. amount withdrawn
   C. anticipated yearly need D. balance on hand

9. Special instructions for storage and release of dated items which are subject to spoilage are LEAST likely needed for

   A. batteries   B. brass couplings
   C. film   D. paint

10. Of the following rodent control measures, the one which is generally LEAST effective is

    A. eliminating sources of food and shelter for the rodents
    B. sealing holes around pipes and wires where rodents may enter the building
    C. setting traps for the rodents
    D. spraying all incoming stock with piperonyl butoxide to kill the rodents

11. Of the following, a well-managed storage operation is MOST likely to reduce the

    A. coordination between purchasing and stores operations
    B. idle time of operating personnel awaiting material
    C. turnover of stored materials
    D. utilization of mechanical aids

Questions 12-21.

DIRECTIONS: Questions 12 through 21 are to be answered SOLELY on the basis of the information given in the following table.

TABLE OF INFORMATION ABOUT GARDEN HOSE ON HAND

Commodity Index Number	Kind and Diameter of Hose (in inches)	Number of Feet Per Roll	Weight Per Roll lbs.	Weight Per Roll ozs.	Cost Per Roll	Number of Rolls on Hand
SL 14171	Plastic, 3/4 in.	25	6	5	5.90	20
SL 14172	Plastic, 3/4 in.	50	12	5	9.90	50
SL 14271	Plastic, 5/8 in.	25	4	7	4.40	40
SL 14272	Plastic, 5/8 in.	50	8	10	7.40	50
SL 14273	Plastic, 5/8 in.	75	13	0	10.40	50
SL 14274	Plastic, 5/8 in.	100	17	0	13.40	100
SL 24171	Rubber, Reinforced, 3/4"	25	9	3	8.90	20
SL 24172	Rubber, Reinforced, 3/4"	50	18	0	14.90	10
SL 24271	Rubber, Reinforced, 5/8"	25	6	2	6.20	40
SL 24272	Rubber, Reinforced, 5/8"	50	12	2	10.90	40
SL 24273	Rubber, Reinforced, 5/8"	75	18	0	15.20	60
SL 24274	Rubber, Reinforced, 5/8"	100	24	0	19.90	100

12. The total number of 25 foot rolls of all types of garden hose currently on hand is   12.____

    A. 120   B. 180   C. 220   D. 400

13. The total weight of one roll each of SL 14172, SL 14273, SL 24271, and SL 24274 is   13.____
    _____ lbs. 7 ozs.

    A. 49   B. 51   C. 55   D. 61

14. The total weight of all of the 25 foot rolls of rubber, reinforced, 5/8 inch garden hose on hand is _____ lbs.   14.____

    A. 175   B. 240   C. 245   D. 485

15. An order for 10 rolls of SL 14271, 17 rolls of SL 14274, and 22 rolls of SL 24271 will MOST NEARLY weigh _____ lbs.   15.____

    A. 333   B. 423   C. 468   D. 472

16. The total cost of 12 rolls of 100 foot plastic, 5/8 inch garden hose is   16.____

    A. $124.80   B. $134.00   C. $160.80   D. $238.80

17. Assume that from the 40 rolls of SL 24272 and the 100 rolls of SL 24274 you ship one order of 10 rolls of SL 24272 and one order of 50 rolls of SL 24274.
    The total cost of all of the SL 24272 and the SL 24274 garden hose still on hand, after filling these orders, is

    A. $479   B. $1,104   C. $1,322   D. $1,451

18. Assume that 15% of all the 100 foot rolls of plastic garden hose and rubber reinforced garden hose are found defective.
    Then, the total cost of the defective hose is

    A. $199.00   B. $298.00   C. $333.00   D. $499.50

19. The stock on hand of which one of the following sizes and types of garden hose has the GREATEST total cost?
    SL

    A. 14171   B. 14271   C. 24171   D. 24172

20. If 3/4 inch plastic garden hose is taken from the 50 foot rolls, then the cost of one foot of such hose is MOST NEARLY

    A. 20¢   B. 23¢   C. 26¢   D. 29¢

21. If it takes one worker one hour to inspect 20 rolls of garden hose for defects, the LEAST amount of time it will take two workers to inspect ALL the rolls of garden hose in stock is _____ hours _____ minutes.

    A. 14; 30   B. 15; 50   C. 24; 10   D. 29; 0

22. Assume that it takes two men forty hours to do a certain job. The time it will take five men to do the same job is _____ hours.

    A. 4   B. 8   C. 10   D. 16

23. Assume that a certain floor covering costs $5.00 per square yard. You order two pieces, one measuring 8 yards by 10 yards and the other measuring 9 yards by 6 yards. The total cost of the two pieces is

    A. $400   B. $570   C. $670   D. $970

24. Assume that you have received a delivery of sand, which took up the entire area of a trailer with interior dimensions of 40 feet by 7 feet and the sand was loaded to an average depth of 4 feet.
    The amount of storage space, in cubic yards, required for this shipment of sand is MOST NEARLY _____ cubic yards.

    A. 42   B. 125   C. 374   D. 1,120

25. Assume that lubricating oil is delivered to your warehouse in 20 gallon drums. Requisitions for amounts less than 20 gallons are filled by drawing off the required amount of lubricating oil from one of the 20-gallon drums. After filling several requisitions for various amounts of lubricating oil, you find that you have on hand 18 full drums, 6 drums that are three-quarters full, 4 drums that are one-half full, and 8 drums that are one-quarter full.
    The total amount of lubricating oil that you have on hand is _____ gallons.

    A. 360   B. 530   C. 540   D. 600

KEY (CORRECT ANSWERS)

1.	D	11.	B
2.	A	12.	A
3.	C	13.	C
4.	C	14.	C
5.	B	15.	C
6.	D	16.	C
7.	A	17.	C
8.	C	18.	D
9.	B	19.	C
10.	D	20.	A

21.	A
22.	D
23.	C
24.	A
25.	B

TEST 2

DIRECTIONS: Each question or incomplete statement is followed by several suggested answers or completions. Select the one that BEST answers the question or completes the statement. *PRINT THE LETTER OF THE CORRECT ANSWER IN THE SPACE AT THE RIGHT.*

Questions 1-13.

DIRECTIONS: Questions 1 through 13 are to be answered by choosing from the given classifications the one under which the item is MOST likely to be found in general stock catalogs.

1. *Chisels* may BEST be classified under

   A. food and condiments
   B. hand tools and accessories
   C. office machines and equipment
   D. stationery supplies

2. *Columnar pads* may BEST be classified under

   A. dry goods, textiles, and floor covering
   B. hospital and surgical supplies
   C. recreational supplies and equipment
   D. stationery and office supplies

3. *Gingham* may BEST be classified under

   A. clothing and textiles
   C. lighting apparatus
   B. hand tools
   D. paints and paint ingredients

4. *Trowels* may BEST be classified under

   A. dry goods and textiles
   B. hand tools and agricultural implements
   C. household supplies
   D. surgical supplies

5. *Collanders* may BEST be classified under

   A. building materials
   C. motor vehicle parts
   B. kitchen utensils
   D. plumbing supplies

6. *Litmus paper* may BEST be classified under

   A. laboratory supplies
   C. stationery and supplies
   B. sewing supplies
   D. textiles

7. *Pipettes* may BEST be classified under

   A. hardware
   B. hospital and laboratory supplies
   C. kitchen utensils and tableware
   D. plumbing fixtures and parts

8. *Carbon tetrachloride* may BEST be classified under 8.____

   A. brushes
   B. clothing and textiles
   C. drugs and chemicals
   D. toilet articles and accessories

9. *Curry powder* may BEST be classified under 9.____

   A. drugs and chemicals
   B. food and condiments
   C. paints and supplies
   D. surgical and dental supplies

10. *Planes* may BEST be classified under 10.____

    A. floor coverings   B. hand tools
    C. household utensils   D. plumbing fixtures

11. *Wing nuts* may BEST be classified under 11.____

    A. food and condiments   B. hardware supplies
    C. household utensils   D. sewing supplies

12. *Chambray* may BEST be classified under 12.____

    A. canned goods, food, and miscellaneous groceries
    B. brooms and brushes
    C. drugs and chemicals
    D. dry goods and textiles

13. *Shears* may BEST be classified under 13.____

    A. agricultural implements B. clothing and textiles
    C. electrical parts   D. furniture

Questions 14-18.

DIRECTIONS: Questions 14 through 18 represent items appearing on requisitions received in a storehouse. Assume that you have a wide variety of each item named. Some important information is missing from each description. Without this missing information (NOT code number or account number), it would be difficult to select the appropriate item from the variety in stock. From the choices given, select the one that represents the missing additional information that would be MOST important and helpful in filling each requisition.

14. PAPER, copy, 100% sulphite sub 20, white 14.____

    A. bond or onionskin   B. ruled or unruled
    C. size of paper   D. two or three holes

15. NEEDLES, hard sewing, 20 to package 15.___

    A. cost B. metallic composition
    C. purpose D. size

16. BATTERY, dry cell, flashlight 16.___

    A. nature of covering B. manufacturer's name
    C. shape of battery D. size of battery

17. SCREWS, wood, gross in box, brass, 1/2", No. 2 17.___

    A. round or flat head
    B. size of bolt
    C. type of lumber for which used
    D. type of metal of which made

18. THREAD, SPOOL COTTON, hand sewing 6 cord, 500 yd., one dozen in box, #60 18.___

    A. color of thread
    B. size of needle's eye
    C. type of fabric to be sewn
    D. diameter of spool

19. If one dozen mops cost $14.00 and one gallon of floor wax costs $10.00, the total cost of five mops and three pints of floor wax is MOST NEARLY 19.___

    A. $9.60 B. $12.00 C. $13.30 D. $14.30

20. Assume that your warehouse issues paint in gallon cans and in quart cans. At the beginning of a certain week, you have 150 gallon cans and 100 quart cans of paint on hand. On Monday, you issue 10 gallon cans and 9 quart cans; on Tuesday, 9 gallon cans and 4 quart cans; on Wednesday, 4 gallon cans and 7 quart cans; on Thursday, 7 gallon cans and 11 quart cans; and on Friday, you issue 5 gallon cans and 5 quart cans.
    The total number of cans of paint on hand at the end of this week, assuming you have received no shipments of paint, is _____ gallon cans and _____ quart cans. 20.___

    A. 35; 36 B. 65; 64 C. 65; 86 D. 115; 64

21. A storage carton with dimensions of 1 foot 6 inches by 2 feet 4 inches by 4 feet has MOST NEARLY a volume of _____ cubic feet. 21.___

    A. 9.33 B. 10 C. 14 D. 15.36

22. Assume that you can purchase a gallon of turpentine for $1.70. A discount of 10% is given for purchases of 80 gallons or more.
    If you purchase 100 gallons of turpentine, the unit cost of one quart of turpentine is MOST NEARLY _____ cents. 22.___

    A. 38 B. 43 C. 77 D. 85

23. Assume that you have dispatched a truck at 9 A.M. to make a single delivery at a location which is 20 miles from your warehouse.
Assuming that the truck travels at an average speed of 15 miles per hour and that one-half is required to make the delivery, you should expect the truck to return to the warehouse at approximately

   A. 10:50 A.M.
   B. 11:40 A.M.
   C. 12:10 P.M.
   D. 12:40 P.M.

23.____

24. Assume that you are informed that on the next day at 9 A.M. you will receive six truck-loads of goods. Two man-hours are required to unload each truckload of goods, and 6 man-hours are required to place each truckload of goods in storage.
If you plan to complete this task by 1:00 P.M., the minimum number of men that you should assign to this task is

   A. 4   B. 8   C. 12   D. 16

24.____

25. Assume that you have in stock 15 one-gallon cans of rubber cement thinner.
After filling an order for 50 bottles each containing 16 fluid ounces of rubber cement thinner, the amount of rubber cement thinner remaining in stock is

   A. none; you do not have enough stock to fill this order
   B. 1 gallon 1 quart
   C. 4 gallons 1 1/2 quarts
   D. 8 gallons 3 quarts

25.____

KEY (CORRECT ANSWERS)

1.	B	11.	B
2.	D	12.	D
3.	A	13.	A
4.	B	14.	C
5.	B	15.	D
6.	A	16.	D
7.	B	17.	A
8.	C	18.	A
9.	B	19.	A
10.	B	20.	D

21. C
22. A
23. C
24. C
25. D

EXAMINATION SECTION
TEST 1

DIRECTIONS: Each question or incomplete statement is followed by several suggested answers or completions. Select the one that BEST answers the question or completes the statement. *PRINT THE LETTER OF THE CORRECT ANSWER IN THE SPACE AT THE RIGHT.*

Questions 1-5.

DIRECTIONS: For Questions 1 through 5, compare the four choices with the number given in the question. Then, select that choice which is exactly the same as the number given.

1. 1201022011

    A. 1201022011 B. 1201020211
    C. 1202012011 D. 1021202011

2. 3893981389

    A. 3893891389 B. 3983981389
    C. 3983891389 D. 3893981389

3. 4765476589

    A. 4765476598 B. 4765476588
    C. 4765476589 D. 4765746589

4. 8679678938

    A. 8679687938 B. 8679678938
    C. 8697678938 D. 8678678938

5. 6834836932

    A. 6834386932 B. 6834836923
    C. 6843836932 D. 6834836932

Questions 6-10.

DIRECTIONS: For Questions 6 through 10, determine how many of the symbols in Column Z are exactly the same as the symbol in Column Y. If NONE is exactly the same, answer A; if only ONE symbol is exactly the same, answer B; if TWO symbols are exactly the same, answer C; if THREE symbols are exactly the same, answer D.

SYMBOL COLUMN Y | SYMBOL COLUMN Z

6. A123B1266

    A123B1366
    A123B1266
    A133B1366
    A123B1266

SYMBOL COLUMN Y	SYMBOL COLUMN Z	
7. CC28D3377	CD22D3377 CC38D3377 CC28C3377 CC28D2277	7.___
8. M21AB201X	M12AB201X M21AB201X M21AB201Y M21BA201X	8.___
9. PA383Y744	AP383Y744 PA338Y744 PA388Y744 PA383Y774	9.___
10. PB2Y8893	PB2Y8893 PB2Y8893 PB3Y8898 PB2Y8893	10.___

11. Which of the following is normally MOST fragile?   11.___

   A. Fresh eggs   B. Iron nails
   C. Steel wool   D. Textbooks

12. Which of the following is normally MOST flammable?   12.___

   A. Aluminum filing cabinets
   B. Automotive gasoline
   C. Raw potatoes
   D. Stainless steel spoons

13. LEGIBLE information entered on a report is information that   13.___

   A. is arranged by ledger account
   B. is numerical
   C. can be read easily
   D. is useful

Questions 14-20.

DIRECTIONS: For each Question 14 through 20, select the choice whose meaning is MOST NEARLY the same as that of the numbered item.

14. ADJACENT   14.___

   A. near   B. critical   C. sensitive   D. sharp

15. AUTHORIZED   15.___

   A. false   B. permitted   C. powerful   D. written

16. DETERIORATE
    A. decorate   B. prevent   C. regulate   D. worsen

17. FLEXIBLE
    A. mixed   B. not expensive   C. not rigid   D. solid

18. NEGLIGENT
    A. careless   B. painful   C. pleasant   D. positive

19. PENDING
    A. awaiting   B. enclosing   C. leaning   D. piercing

20. VENDOR
    A. customer   B. inspector   C. manager   D. seller

Questions 21-24.

DIRECTIONS: Questions 21 through 24 are to be answered SOLELY on the basis of the following passage.

Several special factors must be taken into account in selecting trucks to be used in a warehouse that stores food in freezer and cold storage rooms. Since gasoline fumes may contaminate the food, the trucks should be powered by electricity, not by gasoline. The equipment must be dependable, for if a truck breaks down while transporting frozen food from a railroad car to the freezer of a warehouse, this expensive merchandise will quickly spoil. Finally, since cold storage and freezer rooms are expensive to operate, commodities must be stored close together, and the aisles between the rows of commodities must be as narrow as possible. Therefore, the trucks must be designed to work even in narrow aisles.

21. Of the following, the BEST title for the above passage is
    A. Expenses Involved in Operating a Freezer or Cold Storage Room
    B. How to Prevent Food Spoilage in Freezer and Cold Storage Rooms
    C. Selecting the Best Trucks to Use in a Food Storage Warehouse
    D. The Problem of Contamination of Food by Gasoline Fumes

22. According to the above passage, electrically powered trucks should be used for moving food in freezer and cold storage rooms chiefly because they
    A. are cheaper to operate than gasoline powered trucks
    B. are dependable
    C. can operate in extremes of heat and cold
    D. do not produce fumes which may contaminate food

23. Trucks designed for use in narrow aisles should be used in freezer and cold storage rooms because
    A. commodities are placed close together in freezer rooms to save space
    B. commodities spoil quickly if the space between aisles in the freezer is too wide
    C. narrow aisle trucks are more dependable
    D. narrow aisle trucks are run by electricity

24. According to the above passage, all of the following factors should be taken into account in selecting a truck for use to transport frozen food into and within a cold storage room EXCEPT

    A. ability to operate in extreme cold
    B. dependability
    C. the weight of the truck
    D. whether or not the truck emits exhaust fumes

25. If window glass costs $1.35 per square foot and the cost of installation is 15% of the purchase price of the glass, the total cost of an order, including installation, of 6 panes of glass each measuring 24 inches by 36 inches is

    A. $40.50   B. $46.58   C. $48.60   D. $55.89

KEY (CORRECT ANSWERS)

1. A		11. A	
2. D		12. B	
3. C		13. C	
4. B		14. A	
5. D		15. B	
6. C		16. D	
7. A		17. C	
8. B		18. A	
9. A		19. A	
10. D		20. D	

21. C
22. D
23. A
24. C
25. D

TEST 2

DIRECTIONS: Each question or incomplete statement is followed by several suggested answers or completions. Select the one that BEST answers the question or completes the statement. *PRINT THE LETTER OF THE CORRECT ANSWER IN THE SPACE AT THE RIGHT.*

Questions 1-5.

DIRECTIONS: Questions 1 through 5 show items that have been requisitioned by city agencies. In each group of four items, there is one item which has NOT been described in sufficient detail to enable the stockman to fill the order properly from the variety of stock on hand. For each question, select the item that has pertinent, important information missing.

1. A. Fuses, auto, glass, 25 volts
   B. Ladders, extension, 2 sections, 30', metal
   C. Paint, interior, white, 1 gallon can, flat
   D. Stoppers, rubber, solid, white, nickel plated, brass ring, 1"

2. A. Aspirin, U.S.P., 1 grain - 1000 in bottle
   B. Blotters, desk, 120 lb. stock, 24" x 38", green
   C. Folders, file, manila, 1/3 cut
   D. Nutmeg, ground, 1 lb. container

3. A. Safety pins, brass, nickel plated, size 2
   B. Sheets, bed, cotton, white
   C. Thermometer, oven, 100/600 degree F, enamel
   D. Toothbrush, adult size, nylon bristle

4. A. Pencil, black lead, #2, general office use, with eraser
   B. Stencil, dry-process, blue, legal size #2960
   C. Tape, cellulose, 1/2 in. x 1296 in., core diameter 1 in.
   D. Typewriter ribbon, standard, black record

5. A. Fruits, canned, peaches
   B. Milk, processed, dry powdered, whole, bulk
   C. Olives, stuffed, 16 oz. bottle, 12 bottles to case
   D. Sugar, granulated, 100 lb. bag

6. Assume that in the stockroom you find an assistant stockman in contact with a live electrical conductor and apparently unconscious from shock.
   The FIRST thing that you should do in this case is to

   A. notify your supervisor
   B. see whether the assistant stockman is breathing
   C. send for a doctor
   D. turn off the electric current

7. Of the following, the one which is MOST likely to contribute to accidents involving minor injuries is

   A. careless work practices
   B. insufficient safety posters
   C. lack of safety devices
   D. inexpensive equipment and materials

8. In a stockroom, accidents are often caused either as a result of an unsafe act or an unsafe condition.
   Which one of the following is an example of an unsafe act rather than an unsafe condition?

   A. Lighting that is bright and glaring
   B. Flooring that is well-polished and slippery
   C. Electrical wiring that is frayed
   D. Climbing on shaky boxes to reach a high object

9. Use of materials handling equipment rather than manpower for handling heavy loads generally results in

   A. increased danger of back injuries
   B. increased productivity
   C. reduction of the height of piled materials
   D. reduced productivity

10. On the first morning that you report to work at a new job location as a newly-promoted supervisor of a small unit, your superior asks you what you would like to do FIRST.
    Of the following, the LEAST appropriate response for you to make is to say, *I'd like to*

    A. *meet the employees who work in my unit*
    B. *recommend some changes in the procedures used in my unit*
    C. *obtain a manual of procedure, if one is available*
    D. *see the physical area in which my unit works*

11. As a supervisor, the PRIMARY duty of a stockman is to

    A. accomplish the work assigned to his unit
    B. do more work than any of his subordinates
    C. keep his subordinates busy all the time
    D. know where his subordinates are at all times

12. In teaching new employees how to use forklift equipment, the BEST procedure to follow is:

    A. Give class lecture instruction and then let the employees use the equipment
    B. Let the employees try it themselves and then show them what they are doing wrong
    C. Show the employees how you use the equipment and then answer any questions they may have
    D. Tell the employees how to do it, give a demonstration, have the employees do it, and correct their mistakes

13. Assume that you have assigned one of your assistant stockmen to perform a task involving several steps that he has never done before.
In this situation, of the following, it is generally MOST important for you to

    A. check closely each step in the task as it is being performed or immediately after its completion
    B. make sure that the assistant stockman fully understands the last step before he starts the task
    C. make available to the assistant stockman any tools and equipment that he may request
    D. stress the importance of the task to the assistant stockman

14. When it is necessary to change some work procedures, a supervisor is MOST likely to obtain the cooperation of his subordinates if he

    A. criticizes the procedures followed by his subordinates at present
    B. develops the procedures himself and insists that his subordinates follow the new procedures
    C. informs them that his superior has ordered the subordinates to use the new procedures
    D. involves the subordinates in developing these new procedures

15. Assume that a laborer who has been a disciplinary problem in his previous assignment is transferred to your section. For you, the supervisor, to ask the laborer about his previous problems on the first day that he reports to you for work is generally

    A. *desirable;* it may help you to know how to handle this laborer better
    B. *undesirable,* it may cause the laborer to think that you may be prejudiced against him
    C. *desirable;* it will show this laborer that you are interested in him as an individual
    D. *undesirable;* it may cause your other subordinates to think that you will favor this laborer in work assignments

16. Assume that you, a stockman, have been requested to conduct a ten-hour training course on the operation of the electric lift truck for several newly-appointed assistant stockmen.
Of the following, the MOST important information you would need in order to conduct this training course is the

    A. assistance that you will receive from your supervisor while preparing to conduct this training course
    B. availability of electric lift trucks for use in the training course
    C. educational level of the newly-appointed assistant stockmen whom you will be instructing
    D. hours during the normal work day when the newly-appointed assistant stockmen will be available for the training course

17. Of the following, the FIRST responsibility of a supervisor in a matter which may require disciplinary action is to

    A. call a staff meeting to advise staff what has happened
    B. consult his immediate superior before making an investigation

C. consult various employees individually concerning the matter
D. investigate the matter in an attempt to understand it

18. Assume that a storekeeper has assigned a laborer to assist a stockman in doing a certain task.
The stockman reports to the storekeeper that the laborer has not been doing the work which he, the stockman, has been assigning him.
The MOST appropriate action for the storekeeper to take FIRST in this situation is to

A. direct the laborer to obey the instructions of the stockman
B. have a conference with both the stockman and the laborer present
C. reassign the laborer to another task
D. speak to the laborer to get his side of the story.

19. The one of the following that is an example of an overhead-type handling equipment is

A. handtrucks
B. forklift trucks
C. gravity-roll conveyors
D. chain conveyors

20. Of the following, the advantage of physically inventorying each item only when a requisition for replenishment is made as compared with making a physical inventory of all items once every week is that

A. stealing is more likely to be discovered
B. time spent on counting actual inventory is reduced because of the low level of inventory
C. estimates of replacement costs may be kept fully current
D. all inventory figures are as of a common date

21. When extension forklift arms are added to a forklift truck, the weight carrying capacity of the forklift truck is

A. *decreased*
B. *increased* greatly
C. *increased* slightly
D. *unchanged*

22. Which of the following is NOT an important reason for authorizing a purchasing department to control stores?

A. Coordination of purchasing and stores may result in economies
B. Record keeping of materials in storage is closely associated with the purchase of materials
C. The storage division can inform purchasing of turnover of items to prevent overstocking or understocking
D. The storerooms will be near the points of use, reducing transportation costs

23. When reviewing the operations of a storage facility, of the following, it is LEAST important that the storekeeper review the

A. safety standards being followed
B. utilization of space for storage
C. accuracy of storage records
D. prices used in the preparation of purchase orders

24. A storekeeper in charge of a storehouse has a practice of issuing to only one or two employees the key to the security room where small items of very high dollar value are stored.
   This practice is generally

   A. *desirable;* it prevents items of small value from being placed in the security room
   B. *desirable;* it helps to fix responsibility for safeguarding the items in the security room
   C. *undesirable;* not even the storekeeper in charge should have a key to the security room of a storehouse
   D. *undesirable;* each employee of the storehouse should have a key to the security room

25. Of the following, which one is the MOST important reason for instructing your subordinates to report immediately to you any error or mistake that they have made or discovered?

   A. The subordinate who reports such a mistake or error made by someone else will not be blamed for it.
   B. You may call the mistake to the attention of the person who made it.
   C. You may take appropriate action to correct the error, if required.
   D. You will be able to conceal such mistakes and thereby avoid criticism of yourself or your subordinates.

KEY (CORRECT ANSWERS)

1.	A	11.	A
2.	C	12.	D
3.	B	13.	A
4.	D	14.	D
5.	A	15.	B
6.	D	16.	B
7.	A	17.	D
8.	D	18.	D
9.	B	19.	D
10.	B	20.	B

21.	A
22.	D
23.	D
24.	B
25.	C

CLERICAL ABILITIES

EXAMINATION SECTION
TEST 1

DIRECTIONS: Each question or incomplete statement is followed by several suggested answers or completions. Select the one that BEST answers the question or completes the statement. *PRINT THE LETTER OF THE CORRECT ANSWER IN THE SPACE AT THE RIGHT.*

Questions 1-4.

DIRECTIONS: Questions 1 through 4 are to be answered on the basis of the information given below.

    The most commonly used filing system and the one that is easiest to learn is alphabetical filing. This involves putting records in an A to Z order, according to the letters of the alphabet. The name of a person is filed by using the following order: first, the surname or last name; second, the first name; third, the middle name or middle initial. For example, *Henry C. Young* is filed under *Y* and thereafter under *Young, Henry C.* The name of a company is filed in the same way. For example, *Long Cabinet Co.* is filed under *L*, while *John T. Long Cabinet Co.* is filed under *L* and thereafter under *Long., John T. Cabinet Co.*

1. The one of the following which lists the names of persons in the CORRECT alphabetical order is: 1._____

    A. Mary Carrie, Helen Carrol, James Carson, John Carter
    B. James Carson, Mary Carrie, John Carter, Helen Carrol
    C. Helen Carrol, James Carson, John Carter, Mary Carrie
    D. John Carter, Helen Carrol, Mary Carrie, James Carson

2. The one of the following which lists the names of persons in the CORRECT alphabetical order is: 2._____

    A. Jones, John C.; Jones, John A.; Jones, John P.; Jones, John K.
    B. Jones, John P.; Jones, John K.; Jones, John C.; Jones, John A.
    C. Jones, John A.; Jones, John C.; Jones, John K.; Jones, John P.
    D. Jones, John K.; Jones, John C.; Jones, John A.; Jones, John P.

3. The one of the following which lists the names of the companies in the CORRECT alphabetical order is: 3._____

    A. Blane Co., Blake Co., Block Co., Blear Co.
    B. Blake Co., Blane Co., Blear Co., Block Co.
    C. Block Co., Blear Co., Blane Co., Blake Co.
    D. Blear Co., Blake Co., Blane Co., Block Co.

4. You are to return to the file an index card on *Barry C. Wayne Materials and Supplies Co.* Of the following, the CORRECT alphabetical group that you should return the index card to is   4._____

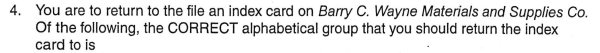

    A. A to G   B. H to M   C. N to S   D. T to Z

Questions 5-10.

DIRECTIONS: In each of Questions 5 through 10, the names of four people are given. For each question, choose as your answer the one of the four names given which should be filed FIRST according to the usual system of alphabetical filing of names, as described in the following paragraph.

In filing names, you must start with the last name. Names are filed in order of the first letter of the last name, then the second letter, etc. Therefore, BAILY would be filed before BROWN, which would be filed before COLT. A name with fewer letters of the same type comes first; i.e., Smith before Smithe. If the last names are the same, the names are filed alphabetically by the first name. If the first name is an initial, a name with an initial would come before a first name that starts with the same letter as the initial. Therefore, I. BROWN would come before IRA BROWN. Finally, if both last name and first name are the same, the name would be filed alphabetically by the middle name, once again an initial coming before a middle name which starts with the same letter as the initial. If there is no middle name at all, the name would come before those with middle initials or names.

Sample Question: A. Lester Daniels
B. William Dancer
C. Nathan Danzig
D. Dan Lester

The last names beginning with D are filed before the last name beginning with L. Since DANIELS, DANCER, and DANZIG all begin with the same three letters, you must look at the fourth letter of the last name to determine which name should be filed first. C comes before I or Z in the alphabet, so DANCER is filed before DANIELS or DANZIG. Therefore, the answer to the above sample question is B.

5. A. Scott Biala
B. Mary Byala
C. Martin Baylor
D. Francis Bauer

5.____

6. A. Howard J. Black
B. Howard Black
C. J. Howard Black
D. John H. Black

6.____

7. A. Theodora Garth Kingston
B. Theadore Barth Kingston
C. Thomas Kingston
D. Thomas T. Kingston

7.____

8. A. Paulette Mary Huerta
B. Paul M. Huerta
C. Paulette L. Huerta
D. Peter A. Huerta

8.____

9. A. Martha Hunt Morgan
    B. Martin Hunt Morgan
    C. Mary H. Morgan
    D. Martine H. Morgan

10. A. James T. Meerschaum
    B. James M. Mershum
    C. James F. Mearshaum
    D. James N. Meshum

Questions 11-14.

DIRECTIONS: Questions 11 through 14 are to be answered SOLELY on the basis of the following information.

You are required to file various documents in file drawers which are labeled according to the following pattern:

DOCUMENTS

MEMOS		LETTERS	
File	Subject	File	Subject
84PM1	(A-L)	84PC1	(A-L)
84PM2	(M-Z)	84PC2	(M-Z)

REPORTS		INQUIRIES	
File	Subject	File	Subject
84PR1	(A-L)	84PQ1	(A-L)
84PR2	(M-Z)	84PQ2	(M-Z)

11. A letter dealing with a burglary should be filed in the drawer labeled

    A. 84PM1   B. 84PC1   C. 84PR1   D. 84PQ2

12. A report on Statistics should be found in the drawer labeled

    A. 84PM1   B. 84PC2   C. 84PR2   D. 84PQ2

13. An inquiry is received about parade permit procedures. It should be filed in the drawer labeled

    A. 84PM2   B. 84PC1   C. 84PR1   D. 84PQ2

14. A police officer has a question about a robbery report you filed. You should pull this file from the drawer labeled

    A. 84PM1   B. 84PM2   C. 84PR1   D. 84PR2

Questions 15-22.

DIRECTIONS: Each of Questions 15 through 22 consists of four or six numbered names. For each question, choose the option (A, B, C, or D) which indicates the order in which the names should be filed in accordance with the following filing instructions:
  - File alphabetically according to last name, then first name, then middle initial.
  - File according to each successive letter within a name.

- When comparing two names in which, the letters in the longer name are identical to the corresponding letters in the shorter name, the shorter name is filed first.
- When the last names are the same, initials are always filed before names beginning with the same letter.

15.
    I. Ralph Robinson
    II. Alfred Ross
    III. Luis Robles
    IV. James Roberts

The CORRECT filing sequence for the above names should be

A. IV, II, I, III   B. I, IV, III, II
C. III, IV, I, II   D. IV, I, III, II

16.
    I. Irwin Goodwin
    II. Inez Gonzalez
    III. Irene Goodman
    IV. Ira S. Goodwin
    V. Ruth I. Goldstein
    VI. M.B. Goodman

The CORRECT filing sequence for the above names should be

A. V, II, I, IV, III, VI   B. V, II, VI, III, IV, I
C. V, II, III, VI, IV, I   D. V, II, III, VI, I, IV

17.
    I. George Allan
    II. Gregory Allen
    III. Gary Allen
    IV. George Allen

The CORRECT filing sequence for the above names should be

A. IV, III, I, II   B. I, IV, II, III
C. III, IV, I, II   D. I, III, IV, II

18.
    I. Simon Kauffman
    II. Leo Kaufman
    III. Robert Kaufmann
    IV. Paul Kauffmann

The CORRECT filing sequence for the above names should be

A. I, IV, II, III   B. II, IV, III, I
C. III, II, IV, I   D. I, II, III, IV

19.
    I. Roberta Williams
    II. Robin Wilson
    III. Roberta Wilson
    IV. Robin Williams

The CORRECT filing sequence for the above names should be

A. III, II, IV, I   B. I, IV, III, II
C. I, II, III, IV   D. III, I, II, IV

20.
    I. Lawrence Shultz
    II. Albert Schultz
    III. Theodore Schwartz
    IV. Thomas Schwarz
    V. Alvin Schultz
    VI. Leonard Shultz

The CORRECT filing sequence for the above names should be

A. II, V, III, IV, I, VI
B. IV, III, V, I, II, VI
C. II, V, I, VI, III, IV
D. I, VI, II, V, III, IV

21.
    I. McArdle
    II. Mayer
    III. Maletz
    IV. McNiff
    V. Meyer
    VI. MacMahon

The CORRECT filing sequence for the above names should be

A. I, IV, VI, III, II, V
B. II, I, IV, VI, III, V
C. VI, III, II, I, IV, V
D. VI, III, II, V, I, IV

22.
    I. Jack E. Johnson
    II. R.H. Jackson
    III. Bertha Jackson
    IV. J.T. Johnson
    V. Ann Johns
    VI. John Jacobs

The CORRECT filing sequence for the above names should be

A. II, III, VI, V, IV, I
B. III, II, VI, V, IV, I
C. VI, II, III, I, V, IV
D. III, II, VI, IV, V, I

Questions 23-30.

DIRECTIONS: The code table below shows 10 letters with matching numbers. For each question, there are three sets of letters. Each set of letters is followed by a set of numbers which may or may not match their correct letter according to the code table. For each question, check all three sets of letters and numbers and mark your answer:
    A. if no pairs are correctly matched
    B. if only one pair is correctly matched
    C. if only two pairs are correctly matched
    D. if all three pairs are correctly matched

CODE TABLE

T	M	V	D	S	P	R	G	B	H
1	2	3	4	5	6	7	8	9	0

Sample Question: TMVDSP - 123456
                            RGBHTM - 789011
                            DSPRGB - 256789

In the sample question above, the first set of numbers correctly matches its set of letters. But the second and third pairs contain mistakes. In the second pair, M is incorrectly matched with number 1. According to the code table, letter M should be correctly matched with number 2. In the third pair, the letter D is incorrectly matched with number 2. According to the code table, letter D should be correctly matched with number 4. Since only one of the pairs is correctly matched, the answer to this sample question is B.

23. RSBMRM 759262
    GDSRVH 845730
    VDBRTM 349713   23.____

24. TGVSDR 183247
    SMHRDP 520647
    TRMHSR 172057   24.____

25. DSPRGM 456782
    MVDBHT 234902
    HPMDBT 062491   25.____

26. BVPTRD 936184
    GDPHMB 807029
    GMRHMV 827032   26.____

27. MGVRSH 283750
    TRDMBS 174295
    SPRMGV 567283   27.____

28. SGBSDM 489542
    MGHPTM 290612
    MPBMHT 269301   28.____

29. TDPBHM 146902
    VPBMRS 369275
    GDMBHM 842902   29.____

30. MVPTBV 236194
    PDRTMB 647128
    BGTMSM 981232   30.____

KEY (CORRECT ANSWERS)

1.	A	11.	B	21.	C
2.	C	12.	C	22.	B
3.	B	13.	D	23.	B
4.	D	14.	D	24.	B
5.	D	15.	D	25.	C
6.	B	16.	C	26.	A
7.	B	17.	D	27.	D
8.	B	18.	A	28.	A
9.	A	19.	B	29.	D
10.	C	20.	A	30.	A

TEST 2

DIRECTIONS: Each question or incomplete statement is followed by several suggested answers or completions. Select the one that BEST answers the question or completes the statement. *PRINT THE LETTER OF THE CORRECT ANSWER IN THE SPACE AT THE RIGHT.*

Questions 1-10.

DIRECTIONS: Questions 1 through 10 each consists of two columns, each containing four lines of names, numbers and/or addresses. For each question, compare the lines in Column I with the lines in Column II to see if they match exactly, and mark your answer A, B, C, or D, according to the following instructions:
- A. all four lines match exactly
- B. only three lines match exactly
- C. only two lines match exactly
- D. only one line matches exactly

	COLUMN I	COLUMN II	
1.	I. Earl Hodgson II. 1409870 III. Shore Ave. IV. Macon Rd.	Earl Hodgson 1408970 Schore Ave. Macon Rd.	1.___
2.	I. 9671485 II. 470 Astor Court III. Halprin, Phillip IV. Frank D. Poliseo	9671485 470 Astor Court Halperin, Phillip Frank D. Poliseo	2.___
3.	I. Tandem Associates II. 144-17 Northern Blvd. III. Alberta Forchi IV. Kings Park, NY 10751	Tandom Associates 144-17 Northern Blvd. Albert Forchi Kings Point, NY 10751	3.___
4.	I. Bertha C. McCormack II. Clayton, MO. III. 976-4242 IV. New City, NY 10951	Bertha C. McCormack Clayton, MO. 976-4242 New City, NY 10951	4.___
5.	I. George C. Morill II. Columbia, SC 29201 III. Louis Ingham IV. 3406 Forest Ave.	George C. Morrill Columbia, SD 29201 Louis Ingham 3406 Forest Ave.	5.___
6.	I. 506 S. Elliott Pl. II. Herbert Hall III. 4712 Rockaway Pkway IV. 169 E. 7 St.	506 S. Elliott Pl. Hurbert Hall 4712 Rockaway Pkway 169 E. 7 St.	6.___

	COLUMN I	COLUMN II	

7.
    I. 345 Park Ave.   345 Park Pl.   7.____
    II. Colman Oven Corp.   Coleman Oven Corp.
    III. Robert Conte   Robert Conti
    IV. 6179846   6179846

8.
    I. Grigori Schierber   Grigori Schierber   8.____
    II. Des Moines, Iowa   Des Moines, Iowa
    III. Gouverneur Hospital   Gouverneur Hospital
    IV. 91-35 Cresskill Pl.   91-35 Cresskill Pl.

9.
    I. Jeffery Janssen   Jeffrey Janssen   9.____
    II. 8041071   8041071
    III. 40 Rockefeller Plaza   40 Rockafeller Plaza
    IV. 407 6 St.   406 7 St.

10.
    I. 5971996   5871996   10.____
    II. 3113 Knickerbocker Ave.   3113 Knickerbocker Ave.
    III. 8434 Boston Post Rd.   8424 Boston Post Rd.
    IV. Penn Station   Penn Station

Questions 11-14.

DIRECTIONS: Questions 11 through 14 are to be answered by looking at the four groups of names and addresses listed below (I, II, III, and IV) and then finding out the number of groups that have their corresponding numbered lines exactly the same.

GROUP I
Line 1. Richmond General Hospital
Line 2. Geriatric Clinic
Line 3. 3975 Paerdegat St.
Line 4 Loudonville, New York 11538

GROUP II
Richman General Hospital
Geriatric Clinic
3975 Peardegat St.
Londonville, New York 11538

GROUP III
Line 1. Richmond General Hospital
Line 2. Geriatric Clinic
Line 3. 3795 Paerdegat St.
Line 4. Loudonville, New York 11358

GROUP IV
Richmend General Hospital
Geriatric Clinic
3975 Paerdegat St.
Loudonville, New York 11538

11. In how many groups is line one exactly the same?   11.____
    A. Two   B. Three   C. Four   D. None

12. In how many groups is line two exactly the same?   12.____
    A. Two   B. Three   C. Four   D. None

13. In how many groups is line three exactly the same?   13.____
    A. Two   B. Three   C. Four   D. None

14. In how many groups is line four exactly the same?   14._____

   A. Two   B. Three   C. Four   D. None

Questions 15-18.

DIRECTIONS: Each of Questions 15 through 18 has two lists of names and addresses. Each list contains three sets of names and addresses. Check each of the three sets in the list on the right to see if they are the same as the corresponding set in the list on the left. Mark your answers:

   A. if none of the sets in the right list are the same as those in the left list
   B. if only one of the sets in the right list is the same as those in the left list
   C. if only two of the sets in the right list are the same as those in the left list
   D. if all three sets in the right list are the same as those in the left list

15.   Mary T. Berlinger   Mary T. Berlinger   15._____
       2351 Hampton St.   2351 Hampton St.
       Monsey, N.Y. 20117   Monsey, N.Y. 20117

       Eduardo Benes   Eduardo Benes
       473 Kingston Avenue   473 Kingston Avenue
       Central Islip, N.Y. 11734   Central Islip, N.Y. 11734

       Alan Carrington Fuchs   Alan Carrington Fuchs
       17 Gnarled Hollow Road   17 Gnarled Hollow Road
       Los Angeles, CA 91635   Los Angeles, CA 91685

16.   David John Jacobson   David John Jacobson   16._____
       178 35 St. Apt. 4C   178 53 St. Apt. 4C
       New York, N.Y. 00927   New York, N.Y. 00927

       Ann-Marie Calonella   Ann-Marie Calonella
       7243 South Ridge Blvd.   7243 South Ridge Blvd.
       Bakersfield, CA 96714   Bakersfield, CA 96714

       Pauline M. Thompson   Pauline M. Thomson
       872 Linden Ave.   872 Linden Ave.
       Houston, Texas 70321   Houston, Texas 70321

17.   Chester LeRoy Masterton   Chester LeRoy Masterson   17._____
       152 Lacy Rd.   152 Lacy Rd.
       Kankakee, Ill. 54532   Kankakee, Ill. 54532

       William Maloney   William Maloney
       S. LaCrosse Pla.   S. LaCross Pla.
       Wausau, Wisconsin 52146   Wausau, Wisconsin 52146

       Cynthia V. Barnes   Cynthia V. Barnes
       16 Pines Rd.   16 Pines Rd.
       Greenpoint, Miss. 20376   Greenpoint, Miss. 20376

18. Marcel Jean Frontenac　　　　　　　　　　Marcel Jean Frontenac　　　　　　18.____
     8 Burton On The Water　　　　　　　　　　6 Burton On The Water
     Calender, Me. 01471　　　　　　　　　　　Calender, Me. 01471

     J. Scott Marsden　　　　　　　　　　　　　J. Scott Marsden
     174 S. Tipton St.　　　　　　　　　　　　　174 Tipton St.
     Cleveland, Ohio　　　　　　　　　　　　　Cleveland, Ohio

     Lawrence T. Haney　　　　　　　　　　　　Lawrence T. Haney
     171 McDonough St.　　　　　　　　　　　　171 McDonough St.
     Decatur, Ga. 31304　　　　　　　　　　　　Decatur, Ga. 31304

Questions 19-26.

DIRECTIONS: Each of Questions 19 through 26 has two lists of numbers. Each list contains three sets of numbers. Check each of the three sets in the list on the right to see if they are the same as the corresponding set in the list on the left. Mark your answers:
   A. if none of the sets in the right list are the same as those in the left list
   B. if only one of the sets in the right list is the same as those in the left list
   C. if only two of the sets in the right list are the same as those in the left list
   D. if all three sets in the right list are the same as those in the left list

19. 7354183476　　　　　　　　　　　　　　7354983476　　　　　　　　　　　19.____
     4474747744　　　　　　　　　　　　　　4474747774
     57914302311　　　　　　　　　　　　　57914302311

20. 7143592185　　　　　　　　　　　　　　7143892185　　　　　　　　　　　20.____
     8344517699　　　　　　　　　　　　　　8344518699
     9178531263　　　　　　　　　　　　　　9178531263

21. 2572114731　　　　　　　　　　　　　　257214731　　　　　　　　　　　　21.____
     8806835476　　　　　　　　　　　　　　8806835476
     8255831246　　　　　　　　　　　　　　8255831246

22. 331476853821　　　　　　　　　　　　331476858621　　　　　　　　　　22.____
     6976658532996　　　　　　　　　　　6976655832996
     3766042113715　　　　　　　　　　　3766042113745

23. 8806663315　　　　　　　　　　　　　　8806663315　　　　　　　　　　　23.____
     74477138449　　　　　　　　　　　　　74477138449
     211756663666　　　　　　　　　　　　211756663666

24. 990006966996　　　　　　　　　　　　99000696996　　　　　　　　　　　24.____
     53022219743　　　　　　　　　　　　　53022219843
     4171171117717　　　　　　　　　　　4171171177717

25. 24400222433004　　　　　　　　　　24400222433004　　　　　　　　　25.____
     5300030055000355　　　　　　　　　5300030055500355
     20000075532002022　　　　　　　　20000075532002022

26. 6111666406600001116   61116664066001116 26.___
   7111300117001100733   7111300117001100733
   26666446664476518   26666446664476518

Questions 27-30.

 DIRECTIONS: Questions 27 through 30 are to be answered by picking the answer which is in the correct numerical order, from the lowest number to the highest number, in each question.

27. A. 44533, 44518, 44516, 44547   27.___
  B. 44516, 44518, 44533, 44547
  C. 44547, 44533, 44518, 44516
  D. 44518, 44516, 44547, 44533

28. A. 95587, 95593, 95601, 95620   28.___
  B. 95601, 95620, 95587, 95593
  C. 95593, 95587, 95601, 95620
  D. 95620, 95601, 95593, 95587

29. A. 232212, 232208, 232232, 232223   29.___
  B. 232208, 232223, 232212, 232232
  C. 232208, 232212, 232223, 232232
  D. 232223, 232232, 232208, 232212

30. A. 113419, 113521, 113462, 113588   30.___
  B. 113588, 113462, 113521, 113419
  C. 113521, 113588, 113419, 113462
  D. 113419, 113462, 113521, 113588

KEY (CORRECT ANSWERS)

1.	C	11.	A	21.	C		
2.	B	12.	C	22.	A		
3.	D	13.	A	23.	D		
4.	A	14.	A	24.	A		
5.	C	15.	C	25.	C		
6.	B	16.	B	26.	C		
7.	D	17.	B	27.	B		
8.	A	18.	B	28.	A		
9.	D	19.	B	29.	C		
10.	C	20.	B	30.	D		

NAME AND NUMBER CHECKING

EXAMINATION SECTION
TEST 1

DIRECTIONS: This test is designed to measure your speed and accuracy. You are urged to work both quickly and accurately and to do correctly as many lists as you can in the time allowed. The test consists of lists of pairs of names and numbers. Count the number of IDENTICAL pairs in each list. Then, select the correct number, 1, 2, 3, 4, or 5, and indicate your choice by circling the corresponding number on your answer paper. Two sample questions are presented for your guidance, together with the correct solutions.

SAMPLE QUESTIONS

CIRCLE
CORRECT ANSWER

SAMPLE LIST A

Adelphi College - Adelphia College
Braxton Corp. - Braxeton Corp.
Wassaic State School - Wassaic State School
Central Islip State Hospital - Central Isllip State Hospital
Greenwich House - Greenwich House

1 2 3 4 5

NOTE that there are only two correct pairs - Wassaic State School and Greenwich House. Therefore, the CORRECT answer is 2.

SAMPLE LIST B
78453694   - 78453684
784530   - 784530
533   - 534
67845   - 67845
2368745   - 2368755

1 2 3 4 5

NOTE that there are only two correct pairs - 784530 and 67845. Therefore, the CORRECT answer is 2.

LIST 1
Diagnostic Clinic   - Diagnostic Clinic
Yorkville Health   - Yorkville Health
Meinhard Clinic   - Meinhart Clinic
Corlears Clinic   - Carlears Clinic
Tremont Diagnostic - Tremont Diagnostic

1 2 3 4 5

LIST 2
73526   - 73526
7283627198   - 7283627198
627   - 637
728352617283   - 728352617282
6281   - 6281

1 2 3 4 5

		CIRCLE CORRECT ANSWER

LIST 3
Jefferson Clinic	- Jeffersen Clinic
Mott Haven Center	- Mott Havan Center
Bronx Hospital	- Bronx Hospital
Montefiore Hospital	- Montifeore Hospital
Beth Isreal Hospital	- Beth Israel Hospital

1 2 3 4 5

LIST 4
936271826	- 936371826
5271	- 5291
82637192037	- 82637192037
527182	- 5271882
726354256	- 72635456

1 2 3 4 5

LIST 5
Trinity Hospital	- Trinity Hospital
Central Harlem	- Centrel Harlem
St. Luke's Hospital	- St. Lukes' Hospital
Mt. Sinai Hospital	- Mt. Sinia Hospital
N.Y. Dispensery	- N.Y. Dispensary

1 2 3 4 5

LIST 6
725361552637	- 725361555637
7526378	- 7526377
6975	- 6975
82637481028	- 82637481028
3427	- 3429

1 2 3 4 5

LIST 7
Misericordia Hospital	- Miseracordia Hospital
Lebonan Hospital	- Lebanon Hospital
Gouverneur Hospital	- Gouverner Hospital
German Polyclinic	- German Policlinic
French Hospital	- French Hospital

1 2 3 4 5

LIST 8
8277364933251	- 827364933351
63728	- 63728
367281	- 367281
62733846273	- 6273846293
62836	- 6283

1 2 3 4 5

LIST 9
King's County Hospital	- Kings County Hospital
St. Johns Long Island	- St. John's Long Island
Bellevue Hospital	- Bellvue Hospital
Beth David Hospital	- Beth David Hospital
Samaritan Hospital	- Samariton Hospital

1 2 3 4 5

LIST 10
62836454	- 62836455	
42738267	- 42738369	
573829	- 573829	
738291627874	- 738291627874	
725	- 735	

CIRCLE
CORRECT ANSWER
1 2 3 4 5

LIST 11
Bloomingdal Clinic - Bloomingdale Clinic
Communitty Hospital - Community Hospital
Metroplitan Hospital - Metropoliton Hospital
Lenox Hill Hospital - Lonex Hill Hospital
Lincoln Hospital - Lincoln Hospital

1 2 3 4 5

LIST 12
6283364728 - 6283648
627385 - 627383
54283902 - 54283602
63354 - 63354
7283562781 - 7283562781

1 2 3 4 5

LIST 13
Sydenham Hospital - Sydanham Hospital
Roosevalt Hospital - Roosevelt Hospital
Vanderbilt Clinic - Vanderbild Clinic
Women's Hospital - Woman's Hospital
Flushing Hospital - Flushing Hospital

1 2 3 4 5

LIST 14
62738 - 62738
727355542321 - 72735542321
263849332 - 263849332
262837 - 263837
47382912 - 47382922

1 2 3 4 5

LIST 15
Episcopal Hospital - Episcapal Hospital
Flower Hospital - Flouer Hospital
Stuyvesent Clinic - Stuyvesant Clinic
Jamaica Clinic - Jamaica Clinic
Ridgwood Clinic - Ridgewood Clinic

1 2 3 4 5

LIST 16
628367299 - 628367399
111 - 111
118293304829 - 1182839489
4448 - 4448
333693678 - 333693678

1 2 3 4 5

CIRCLE
CORRECT ANSWER

LIST 17
    Arietta Crane Farm   - Areitta Crane Farm   1 2 3 4 5
    Bikur Chilim Home   - Bikur Chilom Home
    Burke Foundation   - Burke Foundation
    Blythedale Home   - Blythdale Home
    Campbell Cottages   - Cambell Cottages

LIST 18
    32123   - 32132   1 2 3 4 5
    273893326783   - 27389326783
    473829   - 473829
    7382937   - 7383937
    362890122332   - 36289012332

LIST 19
    Caraline Rest   - Caroline Rest   1 2 3 4 5
    Loreto Rest   - Loretto Rest
    Edgewater Creche   - Edgwater Creche
    Holiday Farm   - Holiday Farm
    House of St. Giles   - House of st. Giles

LIST 20
    557286777   - 55728677   1 2 3 4 5
    3678902   - 3678892
    1567839   - 1567839
    7865434712   - 7865344712
    9927382   - 9927382

LIST 21
    Isabella Home   - Isabela Home   1 2 3 4 5
    James A. Moore Home   - James A. More Home
    The Robin's Nest   - The Roben's Nest
    Pelham Home   - Pelam Home
    St. Eleanora's Home   - St. Eleanora's Home

LIST 22
    273648293048   - 273648293048   1 2 3 4 5
    334   - 334
    7362536478   - 7362536478
    7362819273   - 7362819273
    7362   - 7363

LIST 23
    St. Pheobe's Mission   - St. Phebe's Mission   1 2 3 4 5
    Seaside Home   - Seaside Home
    Speedwell Society   - Speedwell Society
    Valeria Home   - Valera Home
    Wiltwyck   - Wildwyck

LIST 24
		CIRCLE CORRECT ANSWER

LIST 24
63728 - 63738
63728192736 - 63728192738
428 - 458
62738291527 - 62738291529
63728192 - 63728192

1 2 3 4 5

LIST 25
McGaffin - McGafin
David Ardslee - David Ardslee
Axton Supply - Axeton Supply Co
Alice Russell - Alice Russell
Dobson Mfg.Co. - Dobsen Mfg. Co.

1 2 3 4 5

KEY (CORRECT ANSWERS)

1.	3		11.	1
2.	3		12.	2
3.	1		13.	1
4.	1		14.	2
5.	1		15.	1
6.	2		16.	3
7.	1		17.	1
8.	2		18.	1
9.	1		19.	1
10.	2		20.	2

21. 1
22. 4
23. 2
24. 1
25. 2

TEST 2

DIRECTIONS: This test is designed to measure your speed and accuracy. You are urged to work both quickly and accurately and to do correctly as many lists as you can in the time allowed. The test consists of lists of pairs of names and numbers. Count the number of IDENTICAL pairs in each list. Then, select the correct number, 1, 2, 3, 4, or 5, and indicate your choice by circling the corresponding number on your answer paper. Two sample questions are presented for your guidance, together with the correct solutions.

CIRCLE
CORRECT ANSWER

LIST 1

82637381028	- 82637281028
928	- 928
72937281028	- 72937281028
7362	- 7362
927382615	- 927382615

1 2 3 4 5

LIST 2

Albee Theatre	- Albee Theatre
Lapland Lumber Co.	- Laplund Lumber Co.
Adelphi College	- Adelphi College
Jones & Son Inc.	- Jones & Sons Inc.
S.W. Ponds Co.	- S.W. Ponds Co.

1 2 3 4 5

LIST 3

85345	- 85345
895643278	- 895643277
726352	- 726353
632685	- 632685
7263524	- 7236524

1 2 3 4 5

LIST 4

Eagle Library	- Eagle Library
Dodge Ltd.	- Dodge Co.
Stromberg Carlson	- Stromberg Carlsen
Clairice Ling	- Clairice Linng
Mason Book Co.	- Matson Book Co.

1 2 3 4 5

LIST 5

66273	- 66273
629	- 620
7382517283	- 7382517283
637281	- 639281
2738261	- 2788261

1 2 3 4 5

LIST 6
Robert MacColl	- Robert McColl	
Buick Motor	- Buck Motors	
Murray Bay & Co.Ltd.	- Murray Bay Co.Ltd.	
L.T. Ltyle	- L.T, Lyttle	
A.S. Landas	- A.S. Landas	

CIRCLE CORRECT ANSWER
1 2 3 4 5

LIST 7
627152637490 - 627152637490
73526189 - 73526189
5372 - 5392
63728142 - 63728124
4783946 - 4783046

1 2 3 4 5

LIST 8
Tyndall Burke - Tyndell Burke
W. Briehl - W, Briehl
Burritt Publishing Co. - Buritt Publishing Co.
Frederick Breyer & Co. - Frederick Breyer Co.
Bailey Buulard - Bailey Bullard

1 2 3 4 5

LIST 9
634 - 634
162837 - 163837
273892223678 - 27389223678
527182 - 527782
3628901223 - 3629002223

1 2 3 4 5

LIST 10
Ernest Boas - Ernest Boas
Rankin Barne - Rankin Barnes
Edward Appley - Edward Appely
Camel - Camel
Caiger Food Co. - Caiger Food Co.

1 2 3 4 5

LIST 11
6273 - 6273
322 - 332
15672839 - 15672839
63728192637 - 63728192639
738 - 738

1 2 3 4 5

LIST 12
Wells Fargo Co. - Wells Fargo Co.
W.D. Brett - W.D. Britt
Tassco Co. - Tassko Co.
Republic Mills - Republic Mill
R.W. Burnham - R.W. Burhnam

1 2 3 4 5

3 (#2)

CIRCLE
CORRECT ANSWER

LIST 13
   7253529152   - 7283529152
   6283   - 6383
   52839102738   - 5283910238
   308   - 398
   82637201927   - 8263720127

                            1 2 3 4 5

LIST 14
   Schumacker Co. - Shumacker Co.
   C.H. Caiger   - C.H. Caiger
   Abraham Strauss - Abram Straus
   B.F. Boettjer   - B.F. Boettijer
   Cut-Rate Store   - Cut-Rate Stores

                            1 2 3 4 5

LIST 15
   15273826   - 15273826
   72537   - 73537
   726391027384 - 72639107384
   637389   - 627399
   725382910   - 725382910

                            1 2 3 4 5

LIST 16
   Hixby Ltd.   - Hixby Lt'd.
   S. Reiner   - S. Riener
   Reynard Co.   - Reynord Co.
   Esso Gassoline Co. - Esso Gasolene Co.
   Belle Brock   - Belle Brock

                            1 2 3 4 5

LIST 17
   7245   - 7245
   819263728192 - 819263728172
   682537289   - 682537298
   789   - 789
   82936542891   - 82936542891

                            1 2 3 4 5

LIST 18
   Joseph Cartwright - Joseph Cartwrite
   Foote Food Co.   - Foot Food Co.
   Weiman & Held   - Weiman & Held
   Sanderson Shoe Co. - Sandersen Shoe Co.
   A.M. Byrne   - A.N. Byrne

                            1 2 3 4 5

LIST 19
   4738267   - 4738277
   63728   - 63729
   6283628901   - 6283628991
   918264   - 918264
   263728192037 - 2637728192073

                            1 2 3 4 5

LIST 20

		CIRCLE
		CORRECT ANSWER
Exray Laboratories	- Exray Labratories	1 2 3 4 5
Curley Toy Co.	- Curly Toy Co.	
J. Lauer & Cross	- J. Laeur & Cross	
Mireco Brands	- Mireco Brands	
Sandor Lorand	- Sandor Larand	

LIST 21

607	- 609	1 2 3 4 5
6405	- 6403	
976	- 996	
101267	- 101267	
2065432	- 20965432	

LIST 22

John Macy & Sons	- John Macy & Son	1 2 3 4 5
Venus Pencil Co.	- Venus Pencil Co,	
Nell McGinnis	- Nell McGinnis	
McCutcheon & Co.	- McCutcheon & Co.	
Sun-Tan Oil	- Sun-Tan Oil	

LIST 23

703345700	- 703345700	1 2 3 4 5
46754	- 466754	
3367490	- 3367490	
3379	- 3778	
47384	- 47394	

LIST 24

arthritis	- athritis	1 2 3 4 5
asthma	- asthma	
endocrene	- endocrene	
gastro-enterological	- gastrol-enteralogical	
orthopedic	- orthopedic	

LIST 25

743829432	- 743828432	1 2 3 4 5
998	- 998	
732816253902	- 732816252902	
46829	- 46830	
7439120249	- 7439210249	

KEY (CORRECT ANSWERS)

1.	4	11.	3
2.	3	12.	1
3.	2	13.	1
4.	1	14.	1
5.	2	15.	2
6.	1	16.	1
7.	2	17.	3
8.	1	18.	1
9.	1	19.	1
10.	3	20.	1

21. 1
22. 4
23. 2
24. 3
25. 1

CODING

COMMENTARY

An ingenious question-type called coding, involving elements of alphabetizing, filing, name and number comparison, and evaluative judgment and application, has currently won wide acceptance in testing circles for measuring clerical aptitude and general ability, particularly on the senior (middle) grades (levels).

While the directions for this question-type usually vary in detail, the candidate is generally asked to consider groups of names, codes, and numbers, and, then, according to a given plan, to arrange codes in alphabetic order; to arrange these in numerical sequence; to re-arrange columns of names and numbers in correct order; to espy errors in coding; to choose the correct coding arrangement in consonance with the given directions and examples, etc.

This question-type appears to have few parameters in respect to form, substance, or degree of difficulty.

Accordingly, acquaintance with, and practice in the coding question is recommended for the serious candidate.

EXAMINATION SECTION
TEST 1

DIRECTIONS: Questions 1 through 10 are to be answered on the basis of the following Code Table. In this table every letter has a corresponding code number to be punched. Each question contains three lines of letters and code numbers. In each line, the code numbers should correspond with the letters in accordance with the table.

Letter	M	X	R	T	W	A	E	Q	Z	C
Code	1	2	3	4	5	6	7	8	9	0

On some of the lines, an error exists in the coding. Compare the letters and numbers in each question carefully. If you find an error or errors on
  only *one* of the lines in the question, mark your answer A;
  any *two* lines in the question, mark your answer B;
  all *three* lines in the question, mark your answer C;
  none of the lines in the question, mark your answer D.

SAMPLE QUESTION

XAQMZMRQ - 26819138
RAERQEX   - 3573872
TMZCMTZA - 46901496

In the above sample, the first line is correct since each letter, as listed, has the correct corresponding code number.
In the second line, an error exists because the letter A should have the code number 6 instead of 5.
In the third line, an error exists because the letter W should have the code number 5 instead of 6.
Since there are errors in two of the three lines, your answer should be B.

1. EQRMATTR   - 78316443   1.____
   MACWXRQW - 16052385
   XZEMCAR   - 2971063

2. CZEMRXQ   - 0971238   2.____
   XMTARET   - 2146374
   WCEARWEC - 50863570

3. CEXAWRQZ - 07265389   3.____
   RCRMMZQT - 33011984
   ACMZWTEX - 60195472

4. XRCZQZWR - 23089953   4.____
   CMRQCAET - 01389574
   ZXRWTECM - 92345701

5. AXMTRAWR   - 62134653   5.____
    EQQCZCEW   - 77809075
    MAZQARTM   - 16086341

6. WRWQCTRM   - 53580431   6.____
    CXMWAERZ   - 02156739
    RCQEWWME   - 30865517

7. CRMECEAX   - 03170762   7.____
    MZCTRXRQ   - 19043238
    XXZREMEW   - 22937175

8. MRCXQEAX   - 13928762   8.____
    WAMZTRMZ   - 65194319
    ECXARWXC   - 70263520

9. MAWXECRQ   - 16527038   9.____
    RXQEAETM   - 32876741
    RXEWMCZQ   - 32751098

10. MRQZCATE   - 13890647   10.____
    WCETRXAW   - 50743625
    CZWMCERT   - 09510734

———

KEY (CORRECT ANSWERS)

1. D
2. B
3. A
4. C
5. C

6. A
7. D
8. B
9. D
10. A

———

TEST 2

DIRECTIONS: Questions 1 through 6 consist of three lines of code letters and numbers. The numbers on each, line should correspond with the code letters on the same line in accordance with the table below.

Code Letter	F	X	L	M	R	W	T	S	B	H
Corresponding Number	0	1	2	3	4	5	6	7	8	9

On some of the lines, an error exists in the coding. Compare the letters and numbers in each question carefully. If you find an error or errors on
  only *one* of the lines in the question, mark your answer A;
  any *two* lines in the question, mark your answer B;
  all *three* lines in the question, mark your answer C;
  none of the lines in the question, mark your answer D.

SAMPLE QUESTION

  LTSXHMF   2671930
  TBRWHLM   6845913
  SXLBFMR   5128034

In the above sample, the first line is correct since each code letter listed has the correct corresponding number.
  On the second line, an error exists because code letter L should have the number 2 instead of the number 1.
  On the third line, an error exists because the code letter S should have the number 7 instead of the number 5.
  Since there are errors on two of the three lines, the correct answer is B.

1. XMWBHLR   1358924   1._____
   FWSLRHX   0572491
   MTXBLTS   3618267

2. XTLSMRF   1627340   2._____
   BMHRFLT   8394026
   HLTSWRX   9267451

3. LMBSFXS   2387016   3._____
   RWLMBSX   4532871
   SMFXBHW   7301894

4. RSTWTSML   47657632   4._____
   LXRMHFBS   21439087
   FTLBMRWX   06273451

5. XSRSBWFM   17478603   5._____
   BRMXRMXT   84314216
   XSTFBWRL   17609542

6. TMSBXHLS   63781927
    RBSFLFWM   48702053
    MHFXWTRS   39015647

6. ___

KEY (CORRECT ANSWERS)

1. D
2. A
3. C
4. B
5. C
6. D

TEST 3

DIRECTIONS: Questions 1 through 5 consist of three lines of code letters and numbers. The numbers on each line should correspond with the code letters on the same line in accordance with the table below.

Code Letter	P	L	I	J	B	O	H	U	C	G
Corresponding Number	0	1	2	3	4	5	6	7	8	9

On some of the lines, an error exists in the coding. Compare the letters and numbers in each question carefully. If you find an error or errors on
  only *one* of the lines in the question, mark your answer A;
  any *two* lines in the question, mark your answer B;
  all *three* lines in the question, mark your answer C;
  none of the lines in the question, mark your answer D.

SAMPLE QUESTION

JHOILCP 3652180
BICLGUP 4286970
UCIBHLJ 5824613

In the above sample, the first line is correct since each code letter listed has the correct corresponding number.
On the second line, an error exists because code letter L should have the number 1 instead of the number 6.
On the third line an error exists because the code letter U should have the number 7 instead of the number 5.
Since there are errors on two of the three lines, the correct answer is B.

7. BULJCIP   4713920   7.____
    HIGPOUL   6290571
    OCUHJBI   5876342

8. CUBLOIJ   8741023   8.____
    LCLGCLB   1818914
    JPUHIOC   3076158

9. OIJGCBPO 52398405   9.____
    UHPBLIOP 76041250
    CLUIPGPC 81720908

10. BPCOUOJI 40875732   10.____
    UOHCIPLB 75682014
    GLHUUCBJ 92677843

11. HOIOHJLH 65256361   11.____
    IOJJHHBP 25536640
    OJHBJOPI 53642502

KEY (CORRECT ANSWERS)

1. A
2. C
3. D
4. B
5. C

1. D
2. D
3. B
4. A
5. C

KEY (CORRECT ANSWERS)

1. D
2. D
3. B
4. A
5. C

TEST 5

DIRECTIONS: Answer Questions 1 through 6 SOLELY on the basis of the chart and the instructions given below.

Toll Rate	$.25	$.30	$.45	$.60	$.75	$8.90	$1.20	$2.50
Classification Number of Vehicle	1	2	3	4	5	6	7	8

Assume that each of the amounts of money on the above chart is a toll rate charged for a type of vehicle and that the number immediately below each amount is the classification number for that type of vehicle. For instance, "1" is the classification number for a vehicle paying a $.25 toll; "2" is the classification number for a vehicle paying a $.30 toll; and so forth.
In each question, a series of tolls is given in Column I. Column II gives four different arrangements of classification numbers. You are to pick the answer (A, B, C, or D) in Column II that gives the classification numbers that match the tolls in Column I and are in the same order as the tolls in Column I.

SAMPLE QUESTION

Column I	Column II
$.30, $.90, $2.50, $.45	A. 2, 6, 8, 2 B. 2, 8, 6, 3 C. 2, 6, 8, 3 D. 1, 6, 8, 3

According to the chart, the classification numbers that correspond to these toll rates are as follows: $.30 - 2, $.90 - 6, $2.50 - 8, $.45 -3. Therefore, the right answer is 2, 6, 8, 3. The answer is C in Column II.
Do the following questions in the same way.

	Column I	Column II	
1.	$.60, $.30, $.90, $1.20, $.60	A. 4, 6, 2, 8, 4 B. 4, 2, 6, 7, 4 C. 2, 4, 7, 6, 2 D. 2, 4, 6, 7, 4	1.____
2.	$.90, $.45, $.25, $.45, $2.50, $.75	A. 6, 3, 1, 3, 8, 3 B. 6, 3, 3, 1, 8, 5 C. 6, 1, 3, 3, 8, 5 D. 6, 3, 1, 3, 8, 5	2.____
3.	$.45, $.75, $1.20, $.25, $.25, $.30, $.45	A. 3, 5, 7, 1, 1, 2, 3 B. 5, 3, 7, 1, 1, 2, 3 C. 3, 5, 7, 1, 2, 1, 3 D. 3, 7, 5, 1, 1, 2, 3	3.____
4.	$1.20, $2.50, $.45, $.90, $1.20, $.75, $.25	A. 7, 8, 5, 6, 7, 5, 1 B. 7, 8, 3, 7, 6, 5, 1 C. 7, 8, 3, 6, 7, 5, 1 D. 7, 8, 3, 6, 7, 1, 5	4.____

5. $2.50, $1.20, $.90, $.25, $.60, $.45, $.30
    A. 8, 6, 7, 1, 4, 3, 2
    B. 8, 7, 5, 1, 4, 3, 2
    C. 8, 7, 6, 2, 4, 3, 2
    D. 8, 7, 6, 1, 4, 3, 2

6. $.75, $.25, $.45, $.60, $.90, $.30, $2.50
    A. 5, 1, 3, 2, 4, 6, 8
    B. 5, 1, 3, 4, 2, 6, 8
    C. 5, 1, 3, 4, 6, 2, 8
    D. 5, 3, 1, 4, 6, 2, 8

KEY (CORRECT ANSWERS)

1. B
2. D
3. A
4. C
5. D
6. C

TEST 6

DIRECTIONS: Answer Questions 1 through 10 on the basis of the following information:
A code number for any item is obtained by combining the date of delivery, number of units received, and number of units used. The first two digits represent the day of the month, the third and fourth digits represent the month, and the fifth and sixth digits represent the year.
The number following the letter R represents the number of units received and the number following the letter U represents the number of units used.
For example, the code number 120603-R5690-U1001 indicates that a delivery of 5,690 units was made on June 12, 2003 of which 1,001 units were used.

Questions 1-6.

DIRECTIONS: Using the chart below, answer Questions 1 through 6 by choosing the letter (A, B, C, or D) in which the supplier and stock number correspond to the code number given.

Supplier	Stock Number	Number of Units Received	Delivery Date	Number of Units Used
Stony	38390	8300	May 11, 2002	3800
Stoney	39803	1780	September 15, 2003	1703
Nievo	21220	5527	October 10, 2003	5007
Nieve	38903	1733	August 5, 2003	1703
Monte	39213	5527	October 10, 2002	5007
Stony	38890	3308	December 9, 2002	3300
Stony	83930	3880	September 12, 2002	380
Nevo	47101	485	June 11, 2002	231
Nievo	12122	5725	May 11, 2003	5201
Neve	47101	9721	August 15, 2003	8207
Nievo	21120	2275	January 7, 2002	2175
Rosa	41210	3821	March 3, 2003	2710
Stony	38890	3308	September 12, 2002	3300
Dinal	54921	1711	April 2, 2003	1117
Stony	33890	8038	March 5, 2003	3300
Dinal	54721	1171	March 2, 2002	717
Claridge	81927	3308	April 5, 2003	3088
Nievo	21122	4878	June 7, 2002	3492
Haley	39670	8300	December 23, 2003	5300

1. Code No. 120902-R3308-U3300   1.____

   A. Nievo - 12122   B. Stony - 83930
   C. Nievo - 21220   D. Stony - 38890

2. Code No. 101002-R5527-U5007   2.____

   A. Nievo - 21220   B. Haley - 39670
   C. Monte - 39213   D. Claridge - 81927

3. Code No. 101003-R5527-U5007   3.____

   A. Nievo - 21220   B. Monte - 39213
   C. Nievo - 12122   D. Nievo - 21120

4. Code No. 110503-R5725-U5201   4.____

   A. Nievo - 12122   B. Nievo - 21220
   C. Haley - 39670   D. Stony - 38390

5. Code No. 070102-R2275-U2175   5.____

   A. Stony - 33890   B. Stony - 83930
   C. Stony - 38390   D. Nievo - 21120

6. Code No. 120902-R3880-U380   6.____

   A. Stony - 83930   B. Stony - 38890
   C. Stony - 33890   D. Monte - 39213

Questions 7-10.

DIRECTIONS: Using the same chart, answer Questions 7 through 10 by choosing the letter (A, B, C, or D) in which the code number corresponds to the supplier and stock number given.

7. Nieve - 38903   7.____

   A. 851903-R1733-U1703   B. 080502-R1733-U1703
   C. 080503-R1733-U1703   D. 050803-R1733-U1703

8. Nevo - 47101   8.____

   A. 081503-R9721-U8207   B. 091503-R9721-U8207
   C. 110602-R485-U231   D. 061102-R485-U231

9. Dinal - 54921   9.____

   A. 020403-R1711-U1117   B. 030202-R1171-U717
   C. 020302-R1171-U717   D. 421903-R1711-U1117

10. Nievo - 21122   10.____

    A. 070602-R4878-U3492   B. 060702-R4878-U349
    C. 761902-R4878-U3492   D. 060702-R4878-U3492

KEY (CORRECT ANSWERS)

1. D
2. C
3. A
4. A
5. D

6. A
7. D
8. C
9. A
10. A

ARITHMETICAL REASONING
EXAMINATION SECTION
TEST 1

DIRECTIONS: Each question or incomplete statement is followed by several suggested answers or completions. Select the one that BEST answers the question or completes the statement. *PRINT THE LETTER OF THE CORRECT ANSWER IN THE SPACE AT THE RIGHT.*

1. Assume that you have received a delivery of sand, which took up the entire area of a trailer with interior dimensions of 40 feet by 7 feet, and the sand was loaded to an average depth of 4 feet.
   The amount of storage space, in cubic yards, required for this shipment of sand is MOST NEARLY

   A. 42 B. 125 C. 374 D. 1,120

2. Assume that lubricating oil is delivered to your warehouse in 20 gallon drums. Requisitions for amounts less than 20 gallons are filled by drawing off the required amount of lubricating oil from one of the 20 gallon drums.
   After filling several requisitions for various amounts of lubricating oil, you find that you have on hand 18 full drums, 6 drums that are three-quarters full, 4 drums that are one-half full, and 8 drums that are one-quarter full.
   The TOTAL amount of lubricating oil that you have on hand is _____ gallons.

   A. 360 B. 530 C. 540 D. 600

3. Assume that your warehouse issues paint in gallon cans and in quart cans. At the beginning of a certain week, you have 300 gallon cans and 200 quart cans of paint on hand. On Monday, you issue 20 gallon cans and 18 quart cans; on Tuesday, 18 gallon cans and 8 quart cans; on Wednesday, 8 gallon cans and 14 quart cans; on Thursday, 14 gallon cans and 22 quart cans; and on Friday, you issue 10 gallon cans and 10 quart cans. The TOTAL number of cans of paint on hand at the end of this week, assuming you have received no shipments of paint, is _____ gallon cans and _____ quart cans.

   A. 70; 72 B. 130; 128 C. 130; 172 D. 230; 128

4. A storage carton with dimensions of 1 foot 6 inches by 2 feet 4 inches by 4 feet has MOST NEARLY a volume of _____ cubic feet.

   A. 9.33 B. 10 C. 14 D. 15.36

5. A space 5 1/4 feet wide and 2 1/3 feet long has an area measuring MOST NEARLY _____ square feet.

   A. 9 B. 10 C. 11 D. 12

6. One man is able to load two 2 1/2 ton trucks in one hour.
   To load ten such trucks, it will take ten men _____ hour(s).

   A. 1/2 B. 1 C. 2 D. 2 1/2

7. If the average height of the stacks in your section of the storehouse is 10 feet, the area which will be occupied by 56,000 cubic feet of supplies is MOST likely to be

   A. 70' x 80'
   B. 60' x 90'
   C. 50' x 60'
   D. 560' x 100'

8. The number of cartons, each measuring two cubic feet, which can fit into a space which is 100 square feet in area and is 8 feet high is

   A. 50   B. 200   C. 400   D. 800

9. When the floor area measures 200 feet by 200 feet and the maximum weight it can hold is 4,000 tons, then the safe floor load is _____ pounds per square foot.

   A. 20   B. 160   C. 200   D. 400

10. A carton 1' x 1' x 3' measures _____ cubic yard(s).

    A. 1/3   B. 1/9   C. 3   D. 9

11. You have received six cartons, each containing sixty boxes of staples, priced at $72.00 per carton.
    The price per box is

    A. $.60   B. $1.20   C. $7.20   D. $12.00

12. The amount of space, in cubic feet, required to store 100 boxes each measuring 24" x 12" x 6" is

    A. 10   B. 100   C. 168   D. 1,008

13. Assume that it takes an average of two man-hours to stack 1 ton of certain supplies. In order to stack 30 tons, the number of men required to complete the job in ten hours is

    A. 6   B. 10   C. 15   D. 30

14. An area measures 20 feet by 22 1/2 feet. The floor load is 100 pounds per square foot. The total weight that can be stored in this area is MOST NEARLY _____ pounds.

    A. 450   B. 9,000   C. 22,500   D. 45,000

15. The price of a certain type of linoleum is $2.00 per square foot. The total cost of four pieces of 9' x 12' linoleum is MOST NEARLY

    A. $210   B. $800   C. $860   D. $864

16. The number of board feet in a piece of lumber measuring 2 inches thick by 2 feet wide by 12 feet long is

    A. 12   B. 16   C. 24   D. 48

17. If 39 3/8 ounces of a certain commodity are on hand and two requisitions are filled, one for 9 1/2 and one for 9 5/6 ounces, the number of ounces remaining are

    A. 18 2/3   B. 19 1/3   C. 20 1/24   D. 20 3/4

18. In order to fill 96 bottles containing 3 fluid ounces each, the number of pints which would be needed is

    A. 9   B. 18   C. 32   D. 36

19. If a section of a storeroom measures 29 feet by 4 inches by 18 feet 3 inches, the total area is MOST NEARLY _____ square feet.

    A. 523   B. 524   C. 535   D. 537

20. A discount of 1% is given on all purchases of over 100 brushes. An additional discount of 1% is given on all purchases of over 500 brushes.
    If 600 brushes are purchased at a list price of $4.14 each, the total cost is MOST NEARLY

    A. $2,434   B. $2,456   C. $2,460   D. $4,968

21. The following items are purchased: 30 lock sets at $150 per dozen and 10 gross of stove bolts at 15 cents each bolt.
    The total cost is MOST NEARLY

    A. $600   B. $1,800   C. $2,550   D. $4,700

22. The cost of one dozen pieces of screening, each measuring 4'6" by 5', at $.50 per square foot is

    A. $112.50   B. $125.00   C. $135.00   D. $138.00

23. The amount of turpentine on hand is 39 gallons. One requisition is filled for 3 1/2 gallons, three additional requisitions are filled for 3 quarts each, and six requisitions are filled for 1 pint each.
    The quantity of turpentine remaining after all these requisitions have been filled is

    A. 32 gallons   B. 32 gallons 1 quart
    C. 32 gallons 2 quarts   D. 32 gallons 3 quarts

24. A shelf is 30" wide and 20" deep. The shelf is filled solid with 500 boxes, each measuring 2" x 3" x 5".
    The distance from the shelf to the top of the stacked boxes is

    A. 10"   B. 25"   C. 50"   D. 60"

25. In order to check on a shipment of 1,000 articles, a sampling of 100 articles was carefully inspected. Of the sample, one article was wholly defective and 4 more were partly defective.
    On this basis, the percentage of completely acceptable articles in the original shipment is probably MOST NEARLY

    A. 5%   B. 10%   C. 95%   D. 100%

KEY (CORRECT ANSWERS)

1.	A	11.	B
2.	B	12.	B
3.	D	13.	A
4.	C	14.	D
5.	D	15.	D
6.	A	16.	D
7.	A	17.	C
8.	C	18.	B
9.	C	19.	C
10.	B	20.	A

21. A
22. C
23. C
24. B
25. C

SOLUTIONS TO PROBLEMS

1. (40')(7')(4') = 1120 cu.ft. Then, 1120 ÷ 27 ≈ 42 cu.yds.

2. (18)(20) + (6)(15) + (4)(10) + (8)(5) = 530 gallons

3. 300 - (20+18+8+14+10) = 230 gallon cans and 200 - (18+8+14+22+10) = 128 quart cans

4. (1 1/2)(2 1/3')(4') = 14 cu.ft.

5. (5 1/4')(2 1/3') = 12 1/2 sq.ft. ≈ 12 sq.ft.

6. 1 man-hour is needed to load 2 trucks, so 5 man-hours are needed to load 10 trucks. Using 10 men, the time required is $\frac{5}{10} = \frac{1}{2}$ hr.

7. The area = 56,000 ÷ 10 = 5600 sq.ft. The only selection with this area is choice A with 70' by 80'.

8. (100 sq.ft.)(8') = 800 cu.ft. Then, 800 ÷ 2 = 400 cartons

9. (200')(200') = 40,000 sq.ft. Then, 4000 ÷ 40,000 = .1 ton per sq.ft. = 200 lbs. per sq.ft.

10. (1')(l')(3') = 3 cu.ft. = 3/27 cu.yd. = 1/9 cu.yd.

11. 60 boxes = $72.00 means the price per box = $\frac{\$72.00}{60}$ = $1.20

12. (100)(2')(1')(1/2') = 100 cu.ft.

13. 2 man-hours are needed for 1 ton, so 60 man-hours are needed for 30 tons. If 10 hours are used, the number of men needed = 60 ÷ 10 = 6.

14. (100 lbs.)(20')(22 1/2') = 45,000 lbs.

15. (4)($2.00)(9')(12') = $864

16. (2')(12") = 24 sq.ft. per side. For front and back, (24)(2) = 48 sq.ft.

17. 39 3/8 - 9 1/2 - 9 5/6 = 20 1/24 oz.

18. (96)(3) = 288 oz. = 288/16 pints = 18 pints

19. (29 1/3')(18 1/4') = 535 1/3 sq.ft. ≈ 535 sq.ft.

20. 4.14 x 600 = 2484 - (2%) 49.68 = 2434.32

21. ($150X2.5 dozen) + ($.15X1440) = $591 ≈ $600

22. (12)(4 1/2')(5')(.50 per sq.ft.) = $135.00

23. 39 - 3 1/2 - (3)(3/4) - (6)(1/8) = 32.5 gallons = 32 gallons 2 quarts

24. Each level 5" high has 100 boxes
    500 boxes are five 5" levels or 25" high

    ```
              30
         ┌─────────┐
      20 │   100   │
         │ 2x3 boxes│
         └─────────┘
    ```

25. 95 out of a sample of 100 were completely acceptable, so we can assume 950 out of 1000 would be completely acceptable.
    This represents 95%.

TEST 2

DIRECTIONS: Each question or incomplete statement is followed by several suggested answers or completions. Select the one that BEST answers the question or completes the statement. *PRINT THE LETTER OF THE CORRECT ANSWER IN THE SPACE AT THE RIGHT.*

Questions 1-3.

DIRECTIONS: Questions 1 through 3 are based on the following method of obtaining a reorder point: multiply the monthly rate of consumption by the lead time (in months) and add the minimum balance.

1. If the reorder point is 250 units, the lead time is 2 months, and the average monthly rate of consumption is 75 units, then the minimum balance is _____ units.

   A. 75 B. 100 C. 150 D. 250

2. If the lead time is 30 days, the minimum balance is 200 units, and the average monthly rate of consumption is 100 units, then the reorder point is _____ units.

   A. 100 B. 200 C. 300 D. 400

3. If the reorder point is 300 units, the lead time is 2 months, and the minimum balance is 100 units, then the average monthly consumption is _____ units.

   A. 50 B. 100 C. 200 D. 300

4. You are planning to submit an initial order for a new item. You estimate that you will issue 100 per month, and you want to have a two-month supply in reserve.
   You will reorder this item every six months.
   Your initial order should be for

   A. 200 B. 600 C. 700 D. 800

5. For a particular item, the reorder point is established at 585.
   If the average rate of consumption is 130 and the lead time is 3 months, then the amount which should be on hand when the new delivery is received is

   A. 130 B. 195 C. 260 D. 325

6. You have room in the storehouse for 750 cartons of a certain item. Assume that you issue 125 cartons per month and keep a one-month supply in reserve. Delivery time is thirty days.
   Which of the following would it be MOST appropriate to order under these conditions?
   _____ every _____ months.

   A. 250; 3 B. 500; 3 C. 375; 4 D. 500; 4

7. The amount of turpentine on hand is 27 1/2 gallons. One requisition is filled for 3 1/4 gallons, two additional requisitions are filled for 1 quart 8 ounces each, and five requisitions are filled for 2 pints 2 ounces each.
   The quantity of turpentine remaining after all these requisitions have been filled is

   A. 20 gallons, 3 quarts, 1 pint
   B. 21 gallons, 3 quarts, 1 pint
   C. 22 gallons, 1 quart, 6 ounces
   D. 22 gallons, 1 1/2 quarts, 10 ounces

8. If the average height of the stacks in your section of the storehouse is 9 1/2 feet, the area which will be occupied by 11,400 cubic feet of supplies is APPROXIMATELY _____ square feet.

   A. 100   B. 120   C. 1,000   D. 1,200

9. Assume that you have depleted your entire stock of 1,692 units of a certain item by sending 524 units to one location and dividing the remainder of the stock equally among 16 other locations.
   The number of units that was sent to each of these 16 locations was

   A. 48   B. 73   C. 116   D. 168

10. Assume that it takes two men forty hours to do a certain job.
    The time it will take five men to do the same job is _____ hours.

    A. 4   B. 8   C. 10   D. 16

11. Assume that a certain floor covering costs $25.00 per square yard. You order two pieces, one measuring 8 yards by 10 yards and the other measuring 9 yards by 6 yards. The TOTAL cost of the two pieces is

    A. $2,000   B. $2,850   C. $3,350   D. $4,850

12. Assume that your warehouse received a shipment of 600 articles. A sample of 60 articles was inspected. Of this sample, one article was wholly defective and four articles were partly defective.
    On the basis of this sampling, you would expect the TOTAL number of defective articles in this shipment to be

    A. 5   B. 10   C. 40   D. 50

13. The stock inventory card for paint, white, flat, one-gallon, has the following entries:

Date	Received	Shipped	Balance
April 12	-	25	75
April 13	50	75	
April 14	-	10	
April 15	25	-	
April 16	-	10	

    The balance on hand at the close of business on April 15 should be
    A. 40   B. 45   C. 55   D. 65

14. Four city-owned trucks, all the same make, model, and capacity, were dispatched on roundtrips, each with a 20 gallon tankful of gas. After Truck A had traveled 225 miles, his tank was one-quarter full. After Truck B had traveled 120 miles, his tank was half full. After Truck C had traveled 75 miles, his tank was 3/4 full.
    After Truck D had traveled 300 miles, his tank was empty.
    Which truck had the POOREST average mileage per gallon of gas?

    A. A   B. B   C. C   D. D

15. Assume that you receive a shipment of 9 boxes of paper towels. Each box contains 6 dozen packages. Each package contains 200 paper towels. The total cost of the shipment of boxes is $324. The unit of issue for paper towels is the package.
    The unit cost of the paper towels is

    A. $.50 B. $4.50 C. $6.00 D. $36.00

16. One shipment of 70 shovels costs $1,400. A second shipment of 130 shovels costs $2,080.
    The average cost per shovel for both shipments is MOST NEARLY

    A. $16.00 B. $17.50 C. $20.00 D. $25.00

17. Assume that you can purchase a gallon of turpentine for $6.80. A discount of 10% is given for purchases of 80 gallons or more.
    If you purchase 100 gallons of turpentine, the unit cost of one quart is MOST NEARLY

    A. $1.52 B. $1.72 C. $3.08 D. $3.40

18. Assume that you have dispatched a truck at 9 A.M. to make a single delivery at a location which is 20 miles from your warehouse.
    Assuming that the truck travels at an average speed of 15 miles per hour and that one-half hour is required to make the delivery, you should expect the truck to return to the warehouse at APPROXIMATELY

    A. 10:50 A.M. B. 11:40 A.M.
    C. 12:10 P.M. D. 12:40 P.M.

19. Assume that you are informed that on the next day at 9 A.M. you will receive six truckloads of goods. Two man-hours are required to unload each truckload of goods, and 6 man-hours are required to place each truckload of goods in storage.
    If you plan to complete this task by 1 P.M., the MINIMUM number of men that you should assign to this task is

    A. 4 B. 8 C. 12 D. 16

20. Assume that you have in stock 15 one-gallon cans of rubber cement thinner.
    After filling an order for 50 bottles each containing 16 fluid ounces of rubber cement thinner, the amount of rubber cement thinner remaining in stock is

    A. none; you do not have enough stock to fill this order
    B. 1 gallon 1 quart
    C. 4 gallons 1 1/2 quarts
    D. 8 gallons 3 quarts

21. Assume that you have been instructed to order mineral spirits as soon as the supply on hand falls to the level required for sixty days of issue.
    If the total amount of mineral spirits on hand is 960 gallons and you issue an average of 8 gallons of mineral spirits per day, and your warehouse works a five day week, you will be required to order mineral spirits in _____ working days.

    A. 50 B. 60 C. 70 D. 80

22. Assume that a storehouse floor is 300 feet long, 200 feet wide, and 10 feet high. The total weight that the floor can hold is 3,000 tons.
    The safe floor load is _____ pounds per square foot.

    A. 100 B. 200 C. 300 D. 600

23. Seventy cartons, each 2 feet wide, 3 feet long, and 4 feet high, will require storage space measuring APPROXIMATELY _____ cubic yards.

    A. 24 B. 56 C. 63 D. 187

24. A certain item is stored in a crate measuring 3 feet in length, 4 feet in width, and 6 inches in height. It weighs 60 pounds.
    If the usable height of the storage area is twelve feet and if the safe floor load is 140 pounds per square foot, the number of crates which may be stacked right side up in a single column is

    A. 2 B. 5 C. 11 D. 24

25. You have to load 5,000 items on trucks each having a maximum load capacity of 2 1/2 tons. Each item weighs 20 pounds and takes up 2 cubic feet of storage space. Assume that the storage space in each truck has an area of 68 square feet and is 6 feet high. Without exceeding space or weight limitations, the SMALLEST number of trucks that could be used is

    A. 20 B. 25 C. 50 D. 63

KEY (CORRECT ANSWERS)

1. B
2. C
3. B
4. D
5. B
6. D
7. C
8. D
9. B
10. D
11. C
12. D
13. D
14. B
15. A
16. B
17. A
18. C
19. C
20. D
21. B
22. A
23. C
24. D
25. B

SOLUTIONS TO PROBLEMS

1. Let x = minimum balance. Then, (75)(2) + x = 250 Solving, x = 100 units

2. Reorder point = (100)(1 month) + 200 = 300 units

3. Let x = average monthly consumption. Then, (x)(2) + 100 = 300 So, 2x = 200. Solving, x = 100 units

4. Initial order = (2)(100) + (6)(100) = 800

5. Let x = minimum balance. Then, (130)(3) + x = 585 Solving, x = 195 units

6. 750 - 125 = 625. During the 1st month, 125 is issued.
   The 500 cartons left will only last 4 more months, and this would be the appropriate order.

7. 27 1/2 - (l)(3 1/4) - (2)(1 1/4/4) - (5)(2 1/8/8) = 22.296875 gallons = 22 gallons, 1 quart, 6 ounces. [Note: 1 quart = .25 gallons and 6 ounces = 6/128 gallons = .046875 gallons]

8. 11,400 ÷ 9 1/2 = 1200 sq.ft.

9. 1692 - 524 = 1168. Then, 1168 ÷ 16 = 73 units

10. (2)(40) = 80 man-hours. Then, 80 ÷ 5 = 16 hours

11. ($25.00)[(8)(10)+(9)(6)] = $3350

12. 600 ÷ 60 = 10. Then, (10)(5) = 50 defective articles

13. Balance after April 13th = 75 + 50 - 75 = 50. Balance after April 14th = 50 + 0 - 10 = 40. Balance after April 15th = 40 + 25 - 0 = 65

14. Truck A mpg = 225/15 = 15. Truck B mpg = 120/10 = 12.
    Truck C mpg = 75/5 = 15. Truck D mpg = 300/20 = 15.
    So, Truck B had the poorest mpg.

15. (9)(72) = 648 packages of towels. Then, $324 ÷ 648 = $.50 per pkg.

16. ($1400+$2080) ÷ (70+130) = $17.40 ≈ $17.50

17. 100 gallons x 680 = $680 - 10%(68) = 612 ÷ 100 = $6.12 per gallon. $6.12 ÷ 4 = 1.53 quart (closest to $1.54)

18. 20 miles each way requires 20/15 = 1 hr. 20 min., plus 30 min. for delivery. Total time = 3 hrs. 10 min. Finally, 9:00 AM plus 3 hrs. 10 min. = 12:10 PM

19. 8 man-hours are needed for a period of 4 hrs. Thus, 8 ÷ 4 = 2 men per truckload. For six truckloads, 12 men are needed.

20. (50)(16) = 800 oz. = 6 gals. 32 oz. = 6 gals. 1 qt.
    Then, 15 gals. - 6 gals. 1 qt. = 8 gals. 3 qt.

21. 60 ÷ 5 = 12 wks. Then, (12)(40) = 480 gallons. Now, 960 - 480 = 480 gals, and 480 ÷ 8 = 60 working days.

22. (300)(200)= 60,000 sq.ft. Then, 6,000,000 lbs. for 60,000 sq.ft. means 100 lbs. per sq.ft.

23. (70)(2')(3')(4') = 1680 cu.ft. = $62.\overline{2}$ cu.yds. ≈ 63 cu.yds.

24. (3')(4')(140 lbs.) = 1680 lbs. max. weight. Since each item weighs 60 lbs., 1680 ÷ 60 = 28 items could normally be stacked in a single column. However, the max. height allowed is 12 ft., and since the height of each item is 1/2 ft., only 12 ÷ 1/2 = 24 items can be stacked in one column.

25. (2.5)(2000) = 5000 lbs. and 5000 ÷ 20 = 250 max. items per truck by weight. However, (68) (6) ÷ = 204 max. items per truck by space. So, 5000 ÷ 204 ≈ 24.5, and thus 25 trucks will be needed.

ANSWER SHEET

TEST NO. ____________ PART ______ TITLE OF POSITION ______________________________
(AS GIVEN IN EXAMINATION ANNOUNCEMENT - INCLUDE OPTION, IF ANY)

PLACE OF EXAMINATION ______________________________ (CITY OR TOWN) ______________ (STATE) DATE ____________

RATING

USE THE SPECIAL PENCIL. MAKE GLOSSY BLACK MARKS.

1 A B C D E	26 A B C D E	51 A B C D E	76 A B C D E	101 A B C D E
2 A B C D E	27 A B C D E	52 A B C D E	77 A B C D E	102 A B C D E
3 A B C D E	28 A B C D E	53 A B C D E	78 A B C D E	103 A B C D E
4 A B C D E	29 A B C D E	54 A B C D E	79 A B C D E	104 A B C D E
5 A B C D E	30 A B C D E	55 A B C D E	80 A B C D E	105 A B C D E
6 A B C D E	31 A B C D E	56 A B C D E	81 A B C D E	106 A B C D E
7 A B C D E	32 A B C D E	57 A B C D E	82 A B C D E	107 A B C D E
8 A B C D E	33 A B C D E	58 A B C D E	83 A B C D E	108 A B C D E
9 A B C D E	34 A B C D E	59 A B C D E	84 A B C D E	109 A B C D E
10 A B C D E	35 A B C D E	60 A B C D E	85 A B C D E	110 A B C D E

Make only ONE mark for each answer. Additional and stray marks may be counted as mistakes. In making corrections, erase errors COMPLETELY.

11 A B C D E	36 A B C D E	61 A B C D E	86 A B C D E	111 A B C D E
12 A B C D E	37 A B C D E	62 A B C D E	87 A B C D E	112 A B C D E
13 A B C D E	38 A B C D E	63 A B C D E	88 A B C D E	113 A B C D E
14 A B C D E	39 A B C D E	64 A B C D E	89 A B C D E	114 A B C D E
15 A B C D E	40 A B C D E	65 A B C D E	90 A B C D E	115 A B C D E
16 A B C D E	41 A B C D E	66 A B C D E	91 A B C D E	116 A B C D E
17 A B C D E	42 A B C D E	67 A B C D E	92 A B C D E	117 A B C D E
18 A B C D E	43 A B C D E	68 A B C D E	93 A B C D E	118 A B C D E
19 A B C D E	44 A B C D E	69 A B C D E	94 A B C D E	119 A B C D E
20 A B C D E	45 A B C D E	70 A B C D E	95 A B C D E	120 A B C D E
21 A B C D E	46 A B C D E	71 A B C D E	96 A B C D E	121 A B C D E
22 A B C D E	47 A B C D E	72 A B C D E	97 A B C D E	122 A B C D E
23 A B C D E	48 A B C D E	73 A B C D E	98 A B C D E	123 A B C D E
24 A B C D E	49 A B C D E	74 A B C D E	99 A B C D E	124 A B C D E
25 A B C D E	50 A B C D E	75 A B C D E	100 A B C D E	125 A B C D E

ANSWER SHEET

TEST NO. ______________ PART ______ TITLE OF POSITION ______________________________
(AS GIVEN IN EXAMINATION ANNOUNCEMENT - INCLUDE OPTION, IF ANY)

PLACE OF EXAMINATION ______________________________ (CITY OR TOWN) ______________ (STATE) DATE ______________

RATING

USE THE SPECIAL PENCIL. MAKE GLOSSY BLACK MARKS.

1 A B C D E	26 A B C D E	51 A B C D E	76 A B C D E	101 A B C D E
2 A B C D E	27 A B C D E	52 A B C D E	77 A B C D E	102 A B C D E
3 A B C D E	28 A B C D E	53 A B C D E	78 A B C D E	103 A B C D E
4 A B C D E	29 A B C D E	54 A B C D E	79 A B C D E	104 A B C D E
5 A B C D E	30 A B C D E	55 A B C D E	80 A B C D E	105 A B C D E
6 A B C D E	31 A B C D E	56 A B C D E	81 A B C D E	106 A B C D E
7 A B C D E	32 A B C D E	57 A B C D E	82 A B C D E	107 A B C D E
8 A B C D E	33 A B C D E	58 A B C D E	83 A B C D E	108 A B C D E
9 A B C D E	34 A B C D E	59 A B C D E	84 A B C D E	109 A B C D E
10 A B C D E	35 A B C D E	60 A B C D E	85 A B C D E	110 A B C D E

Make only ONE mark for each answer. Additional and stray marks may be counted as mistakes. In making corrections, erase errors COMPLETELY.

11 A B C D E	36 A B C D E	61 A B C D E	86 A B C D E	111 A B C D E
12 A B C D E	37 A B C D E	62 A B C D E	87 A B C D E	112 A B C D E
13 A B C D E	38 A B C D E	63 A B C D E	88 A B C D E	113 A B C D E
14 A B C D E	39 A B C D E	64 A B C D E	89 A B C D E	114 A B C D E
15 A B C D E	40 A B C D E	65 A B C D E	90 A B C D E	115 A B C D E
16 A B C D E	41 A B C D E	66 A B C D E	91 A B C D E	116 A B C D E
17 A B C D E	42 A B C D E	67 A B C D E	92 A B C D E	117 A B C D E
18 A B C D E	43 A B C D E	68 A B C D E	93 A B C D E	118 A B C D E
19 A B C D E	44 A B C D E	69 A B C D E	94 A B C D E	119 A B C D E
20 A B C D E	45 A B C D E	70 A B C D E	95 A B C D E	120 A B C D E
21 A B C D E	46 A B C D E	71 A B C D E	96 A B C D E	121 A B C D E
22 A B C D E	47 A B C D E	72 A B C D E	97 A B C D E	122 A B C D E
23 A B C D E	48 A B C D E	73 A B C D E	98 A B C D E	123 A B C D E
24 A B C D E	49 A B C D E	74 A B C D E	99 A B C D E	124 A B C D E
25 A B C D E	50 A B C D E	75 A B C D E	100 A B C D E	125 A B C D E